This book is dedicated to every teacher who loves to teach but hates all the crap that comes with it...

The (Un)official Teacher's Manual:

What They Don't Teach You at Training College

By Omar Akbar

Contents

Introduction:

Why This Book Was Written

Whatever your route into teaching, there are some things they just didn't teach you and you weren't at any school long enough to pick them up via osmosis. Teacher training courses tell you how to teach, but there is a whole other set of rules (and guidance) which will not only help you to reach your full potential as a teacher, but also help you to avoid the pitfalls which you don't even realise exist until you're ass-deep in them. Be assured that there is absolutely no pedagogy in this book whatsoever, as countless books have been written on that. Why would I waste every Sunday for an entire year writing a book on something you already know and are constantly learning about? Hell no. I'm a teacher, my time is scarce. Anything I do in my spare time must either be fun, or in some way beneficial. In this case the beneficiary is you.

Whether you're merely considering a teaching career, a trainee teacher, or an experienced teacher, you'll benefit from the not-so-obvious advice included in this book. The (Un)official Teacher's Manual will tell you:

- How to get the most from lesson observations, learning walks and book scrutinies
- How not to write a school email
- How to get promoted (if you want to!)
- When and how to say no and yes
- What to do and not do during meetings
- How to get parents on your side
- How to thrive and avoid the pitfalls of teacher training
- How to ensure a life-work balance
- How to identify, avoid and handle school bullies

- How to get the teaching job you want
- How to maintain good relationships at school
- Why it IS all worth it

After 11 years, 5 months and 4 schools of teaching, dozens of training courses, conferences and so on, one thing I am certain of is this: there is no guidance (or very little guidance) for teachers on the preceding topics and there is a dire need for it. I have never spoken to a teacher who received guidance on how to manage a 53+ hour working week, and I've never known a teacher who was taught how to send a school email. I have however seen many teachers getting in trouble for saying the wrong thing in a meeting, or not getting promoted when they're certain they should be. Guidance in these and similar areas is not only beneficial but imperative.

Some of the contents of this book I have learnt from my own mistakes, but most of it is what I have observed time and time and time again, in multiple schools, staffrooms and conferences. Schools may differ from each other, but the teaching profession is still the teaching profession and while you may have to adapt what you read to your own specific school and your own individual life, consider The (Un)official Teacher's Manual as necessary as any professional development session you've ever attended.

The protection of your happiness, savviness, and success are at the heart of this book and I hope I deliver on this intent. Be aware however, that no punches have been pulled: I have been direct in my advice and there are things in this book that you will not like the sound of. There are also, however, things that will make you realise and appreciate the rewards of a teaching career. I ask that you maintain a holistic view and not jump to conclusions about people or the profession based on chapters read in isolation. Good luck, fellow teachers!

1.

How to Get the Most From Observations, Learning Walks, and Book Scrutinies

Observations

Tips for success

You receive an email. You rush and check your calendar. You look at your scheme of work to find out what topic you will be teaching. You become slightly preoccupied and begin talking to people about pedagogy, literacy, numeracy, and you may even begin to doubt your teaching ability. This can only mean one thing: you are having a lesson observation very soon.

Now there are countless books about teaching methods from which we have all benefited, all with the noble intention of improving our teaching. As stated previously, the aim of this is book is not to rehash the *Teacher's Toolkit.* This section deals with the not-so-obvious side of lesson observations and how to succeed and avoid disasters.

Firstly, it is imperative that you stick to your school's interpretation of Ofsted criteria. Be mindful of this, particularly if you have taught in other schools, as there are subtle (and indeed not-so-subtle) ways in which schools vary in what is required in a lesson for a particular grade. If your school requires you to differentiate by graded outcomes to get graded as 'good', then act accordingly. If your school wants to see marking every six lessons in books to get a 'good' grade then make sure it is there. Regardless of how much your friends at other schools don't have to do all the things that you have to do, and as against your nature as it sounds, do as you're told and stick to the interpretation of your school. At times, schools are of the impression that their interpretation is the only correct interpretation, and everyone else's is either wrong or inferior. Keep your maverick tendencies hidden this time.

Secondly, be sure to show an attitude of wanting to be successful in the observation. Obvious? Of course it is, but what I mean is this: your teaching is being judged on your observation, no matter how much it is said or indicated otherwise. The fact is that in the eyes of your leadership team, you are as good as your most recent observation; it doesn't matter how many previous 'good' observations you have had as they are not in the present. I mention this because when an observation goes wrong, teachers often defend themselves by arguing that they got an 'outstanding' in the last one. Unfortunately, while they may be right, this does not let them off the hook – more about this later. It is therefore a good idea to show your observer and your line managers that you are taking the observation seriously and that you want to do well. Statements such as 'I want them to see me at my best' or something similar will give people a good impression of you before the observation. Make it obvious that you are preparing thoroughly. Perhaps ask somebody to check your lesson plan and make sure it is detailed, fulfils criteria and so on. If it is known that you are trying, you will subconsciously be graded positively before the observation even begins.

Having said this, do be careful: if you are spending the week before your observation coming into school early, marking books, cutting up cards, printing off success criteria, and generally making it quite obvious that you do not normally plan to anywhere near the same extent as you are for your observation, middle leaders will sense this and you will lose credibility in their eyes. Even the most seemingly oblivious middle leader is always making quiet judgements on your practice even though they are not in the classroom with you. Appear to desire success, but don't behave as if it's the first ever time you've decided to care about how good your teaching is.

Thirdly, make sure there are no surprises: if you have never differentiated by outcome, never done card sorts, role plays, traffic lights, or pretty much anything else, do not wait for your observation to try it out! It is common for observers to ask pupils about the lesson and whether or not it's radically different from others. If you're bullshitting you will get caught, and even if you don't, a totally new teaching activity or style is likely to make you even more nervous and you run the risk of making mistakes while in a state of panic. In addition to this, your class may behave unpredictably and this will only add to your tension. If you do decide to be daring, then try the activity in the lessons leading up to your observation so that it's not entirely new for you or the kids. Of course, the aforementioned issues are minimised when you try your best for the kids on a regular basis: this is part and parcel of being a good teacher. Try and get to a point in your career where you couldn't care less what the observers think because you and the kids know you do them proud day in and day out.

Fourthly, be aware of your observer(s): obviously you will know who they are, but do you know what they like to see in lessons? For example, if you're being observed by the Head of Literacy then it's probably a good idea to have some literacy activities in your lesson. If you're a trainee/NQT then your observer will want to see some of the ideas they have suggested, so it's important you show that you are following them. It is a good idea to subtly find out (or infer) what your observer likes to see in lessons and demonstrate this. Be careful though: you don't have to completely ditch your own great ideas and end up in the disaster zone described earlier, but a pinch of what they want is always a good idea.

If it goes wrong: what to do and what definitely not to do

You spent ages planning your lesson. You had the plan checked by two different people. You had all resources and paperwork intact, but for one reason or other you did not carry it off on the day. You feel like you're about to be executed. You cannot believe this is happening to you. They're looking you dead in the eye; their faces slightly disgruntled with mild disrespect as if you just left the toilet without washing your hands. You sit timidly awaiting your feedback, and then comes the dreaded 'How do you think it went?' line of questioning. Then you hear those horrible phrases, 'requires improvement', 'inadequate', and you feel like you want to throw the desk over and scream swear words at the top of your voice. You want to accuse the observer(s) of being in the wrong and inform them that they are shit anyway and they shouldn't be telling you what to do. Obviously, that would do your career no favours! So what would help? Here's some advice on what to do when it all goes wrong:

Hyperbole aside, you absolutely, positively, must ignore the tendency to get defensive. When the dreaded question comes, you must, must, *must* call a bad lesson a bad lesson.

After having admitted to that, it's essential that you give the exact breakdown of how and where it went wrong, and what you would do differently next time. Also, you must not blame external factors: don't say you didn't have time to plan it or to mark your books (even if it's true). All of these behaviours, to the observer, will convey that not only are you incompetent, but you are *unconsciously* incompetent, which is the worst type of incompetence. You must have an 'I put my hands up, it was my fault' attitude throughout the feedback session and make sure you mention the shortcomings before they do. Take advantage of that first question: if you've already grilled yourself, they won't grill you again (at least not as much). Depending on your school, they're likely to want to reobserve you, and may even put you on some sort of coaching program. If you feel you don't need the coaching then decline politely, not defensively. You may want to mention your excellent track record and it's fine to do so, but don't over do it, as it will not be your saving grace.

Appear eager to be observed again, as difficult as it may be. Remember that the more bothered you are by your lesson going wrong, the less they will be. A failing member of staff is a liability and the less work you create for them the better it is for both parties.

When you disagree with the judgement

The grading and overall judgement of a lesson is very subjective. Different observers put an emphasis, consciously or unconsciously, on different criteria. Personally I am more likely to favour a lesson that shows obvious pupil engagement and a positive relationship with the teacher over a lesson that shows 'rapid and sustained' pupil progress. It's apples and oranges. In most schools today, observations are conducted by two members of staff, so there is a potential for three different opinions (although these are unlikely to radically differ).

At some stage in your career you will be given a judgment that you disagree with, usually because it should be higher in your eyes. There are many reasons for being given an 'unfair' judgement, but the two most common reasons are: firstly, because you are being bullied (more about this later), and secondly because your observer has interpreted Ofsted criteria differently to you, and both of you believe that you are correct and that the other person is incorrect.

In most situations, no matter how much you argue, your grade will not be changed. Why? Well, it's for the same reason that you don't let your pupils get away with misbehaviour, irrespective of who they are: if you let one get away with it, they will all get away with it. If you are newish to the profession the advice on disagreeing with a judgement is simple: don't! Or at least if you do, don't expect to win.

However, if you are an established member of staff or a daring NQT and you decide to fight your case, take note of the advice that follows:

All too many teachers argue incorrectly, which usually means defensively and emotionally. Do not go in there all guns blazing saying 'There is no possible way that was only a 'good'. I've never been anything less than outstanding for the past 5 years and I've done those activities before and got an outstanding. You two blatantly don't know what an outstanding lesson looks like! I'm better than both of you! How dare you down-grade me?!'

This is not likely to change their minds. Instead, refer to the same criteria that you believe they are misinterpreting; be calm but assertive, and never make a point unless you can back it up with evidence from what happened in your lesson combined with the grading criteria. Saying something to the effect of 'I would grade the lesson as outstanding as it was clear that the pupils made progress beyond their target grade' would be far more effective, and even if it doesn't change their mind, you will show the observer that you at least *tried* for a high grade the best way you know how.

A note to observers

I can recall a time during the first summer after 9/11 when I was stopped by U.S. Customs agents at Chicago O'Hare International Airport while I was on my way to Seattle. As soon as I got to the front of the customs queue, there were two of them, both with guns. The agents took my passport and put me in a room with others of, let's just say, a similar physical description. Every now and again I would walk over to the desk and ask the agent (a third one with a gun) what exactly the problem was, and when I would be released. He would just say 'Wait here, sir'. There was no rhyme or reason. I waited in that room for a total of four hours and when they finally released me I missed my connecting flight.

Being observed feels worse than I felt that day. Teachers hate being observed. They get nervous. They sweat and stammer. They feel as if they are guilty unless proven innocent. They want it to finish but it just doesn't seem to. They want to know how it's going, but their anxiety shuts down their instincts.

It's an awkward, horrible feeling. You will most probably get to observe somebody's lesson at an early stage in your career, for whatever reason, and to this end here are some suggestions which will help you to be recognised as a well reasoned, positive observer who everyone is comfortable around.

Firstly, aim to put people at ease: so many observers have a plain look of death on their face while observing and this can be very off-putting for the observee! It's a good idea to smile as you see the good practice happening in real time. The teacher will be very aware of your body language and so shaking your head or looking disgruntled (even if you have reason to) will be counterproductive to a good lesson. So smile! If it's not in your nature to smile and you prefer being a plain-faced observer, try not to stare directly at the teacher as plain-faced eye-to-eye staring could be construed as aggressive and therefore put the teacher on edge. If you think this advice is a bit too touchy-feely then tell the teacher quietly at the start of the lesson 'Ignore me, I tend to look very serious when observing. It doesn't mean anything'. On the other hand, if you believe no sympathy whatsoever should be shown to the observed teacher, then do us all a favour and leave the profession.

Secondly, don't be pernickety; be holistic. You won't gain many friends if you're that one person who looks at everything on the observation criteria sheet, analyses every small section in detail and has 15 minutes of feedback on how the teacher should have used a different font for their PowerPoint presentation. Get over yourself and look at the bigger picture. It's a lesson observation, not a driving test. Don't be on a mission to search for the three minor faults by which you are going to fail them. It's just not necessary.

Thirdly, be very positive during the feedback. I remember many years ago after observing my lesson, a Deputy Head said 'If you were my son's chemistry teacher, I'd be overjoyed'. It was a holistic comment personal in nature. Compare this to 'Your AfL was good'. Doesn't exactly get your endorphins pumping does it? I walked away from that observation with confidence and an increased desire to improve. Do you want to be someone who makes people want to do better? Or do you want be someone who makes people see the observation process as a box-ticking exercise, and as long as they get you off their ass it's ok? Be very positive about the positives you observe.

Learning Walks

What they are and what to do about them

You will most likely be experiencing regular learning walks. These are when someone, usually a middle or senior leader, drops into your lesson for a few minutes and leaves. They may have a clipboard where they take notes or fill out a checkbox sheet, and they may talk to pupils or look at their books. It's often stated that the reason for learning walks is to get a snapshot of what goes on in your classroom on a daily basis. For the most part, learning walks are inoffensive, unobtrusive and innocent, however it ultimately depends on how your school is run. In any case, the fact of the matter is this: If you observe any teacher often enough, you will catch them out eventually. This is the primary reason why teachers cannot help but feel some degree of anxiety when someone comes to watch their lesson, irrespective of the time duration. Even the most enthusiastic, all singing, all dancing teacher will occasionally be snowed under with work and find it necessary to tell their class to work from books while they catch up on their marking. It's just part and parcel of a 50+ hour working week.

Sometimes learning walks are announced, in which case just treat it as a mini observation and follow the guidelines in the previous section. It is however becoming increasingly common to not announce learning walks, in which case more specific advice is needed. Hopefully the following guidance will help you to achieve a successful learning walk.

Firstly, it's a good idea to be aware of who does learning walks and when. For example, if you're a secondary school teacher, then your Head of Department will most likely be conducting learning walks. Find out when their free periods are and make sure your lessons show whatever it is your school is looking for at that time. This is not entirely foolproof as very often senior leaders conduct learning walks, and they are almost always free when you are teaching. If this is the case, then look for patterns. For example, at one school it became obvious that Friday morning was the Assistant Head's favourite or most convenient time to conduct learning walks, so staff made sure not to catch up on paperwork in those lessons. It goes without saying that no teacher should make a habit of this anyway, even if they can get away with it, as doing so would be a gross disservice; this advice is for those times when you absolutely have no choice. Senior leaders often do different departments on different days or do different sections of the school at different times in a day. It's useful to talk to your friends in other departments to find out if there are any Assistant Heads lurking.

It would be both ridiculous and destructive to your mental health if you had to engage in a *Crystal Maze* style treasure hunt to try and avoid being caught out every time you hear about a learning walk. Try not to get too paranoid and be confident in your daily practice. Chapter 8 will help you plan your time better, so you are more likely to be free from doing paperwork in the classroom and therefore be at your best as much as possible.

If it goes wrong: what to do and what definitely not to do

When speaking about learning walks, statements such as 'We're not watching you, we're watching the kids', 'We're looking at the progress in the lesson, not the teaching' or 'It's about the learning not the teaching' are often used. Such statements are well-meaning but inadvertently deceptive. Allow me to explain: strictly speaking, the focus of Ofsted is indeed now on pupil progress, this part is true. But the reason you are told the above is primarily to put you at ease by indicating that the pressure is not on you but on the pupil. Now, there may be some pressure on the pupil, as they are the ones who have to perform, but the simple fact is that if your learning walk goes wrong, it is you that suffers the consequences. Do not be fooled. If you end up in a middle leader's office after a disaster of a learning walk, saying 'I thought you were watching the kids!' will get you nowhere.

A learning walk can go wrong for a number of reasons and I'm sure we can all list a few. But it's what you do afterwards that is going to be crucial to your professional reputation or even your career progression. Here are some tips:

Whether you were sitting at the front checking your email while your class were doing a mundane book task, or your books weren't marked, the protocol is the same. Firstly, find out what is being done with the information from your learning walk and insist on an answer. Ask questions: Who is seeing the notes? Are they going to be filed away with your name next to them? Will it affect your performance management? Once you have demanded answers to these questions, and even if you are satisfied that this learning walk will not be used to against you in future, request another learning walk anyway. Yes, request another one. Why? For the simple reason that even if notes are not being made and recorded physically, the mental notes will remain in the observer's mind for a long time unless you do something to neutralise them. It doesn't matter how laid back the observer seemed, the notes exist in one format or another. It's only a 10 minute drop in; do what you can to undo it. A simple 'Would you be able to come back next week? I've had such a busy week and I've been a bit behind', or something similar, will suffice. Even if they insist it's not necessary or no big deal, observers often perform another learning walk on weaker (or perceived weaker) teachers. Stay ahead of the game. If you are wrong, and it really is no big issue, then at least you will be respected because you care about how your teaching is perceived.

Book Scrutinies

Your school may have a different name for it: book scrutiny, book look, book check or even feedback analysis. The purpose is the same: to make sure you are marking your books in accordance with school policy. I can recall reading Sue Cowley stating that marking is a 'balancing act'. Nothing could be more true. No teacher, at any stage in their career, can hand on heart say that they are up to date with all of their marking, at any point in the school year. The most you can ever do is manage marking; teachers can never master marking. Just like lesson observations and learning walks, it is important to realise that your entire marking will be judged upon the marking that is observed during a book scrutiny. It is imperative therefore that you get it right. While you may never master the art of marking, you can master the art of having a successful book scrutiny if you follow this guidance.

Make it obvious

Your school will most likely want you to follow a particular policy and mark in a certain way, and this will usually involve some sort of feedback from the pupil, for example pupil dialogue. Make sure that it is absolutely evident from your books that you are following the policy; your marking must stand out in your books. Whoever is checking is likely to be pressed for time and wants to get their boxes ticked quickly without avoidable obstacles. For example, if your class has many worksheets stuck in the book, and you have marked those worksheets, make sure the worksheets are not folded and thereby hiding your marking! When you do self assessment (SA) and peer assessment (PA) in your lessons, make sure the pupils use a different coloured pen and write SA and PA in the margin. If you are doing a practical, get pupils to write 'Practical' as a sub-heading. The latter may well be part of your marking policy, but if it isn't, do it anyway. During a book scrutiny, always assume, albeit cynically, that if they can't see it, they will assume you are not doing it and thus scrutinise you further. However, try not to let this type of cynicism put you in a negative frame of mind. Just see it as a game that needs to be played.

When you don't have the books

Often school leaders ask for the books of individual pupils as well as, or instead of, whole class sets. In light of this, it is easily possible for the books not to be in your possession when asked for, as you may have given them to the pupils themselves to revise for a test, or that particular pupil may have lost their book (to name a few possibilities!). It is surprisingly common for these variables not to be factored in when asking for books so a backup plan is advised.

Firstly, explain to the checker that you don't have those specific books and instead give them some books that you do have, which match the description of the pupils they want to see. For example, a Head of Department may ask to check the books of three named pupils, one on target, one above and one below. For whatever reason, you don't have the books. After apologising for not having them, give them books of other pupils who match these descriptions instead. Never show up to a book scrutiny with nothing but an excuse, as all you'll do is invite more scrutiny. Playing the game is necessary here also.

When you haven't marked the books

Depending on your school, the notice you get given for a book scrutiny, if any, will vary. There's always a chance then that you may be behind on marking and don't have the time to be up to date for the scrutiny. In this case, the only thing you can do is apologise, provide an alternative, and then rectify. For example, if you are asked for year 8 books and you haven't marked them, but you have marked year 11, say something to the effect of 'I'm sorry but my time has been taken up with my year 11 as they are a priority group. I'm very behind on my year 8 but I've got my year 11s if you'd like to have a look? I can get the year 8s done by next week if that's ok?'

By doing this, you are showing the checker that you aren't lazy, your time has been spent elsewhere and you just got caught up is all. Being willing to apologise, explain and provide an alternative will at least put you in a good light. Even if it isn't fully accepted, you will at least lessen the damage to your professionalism. Just don't make a habit of it.

And finally, beware of snoopers

Every school has them. They come in all shapes and sizes, personalities, and positions within a school. Snoopers are staff who check your marking without your knowledge.

This normally happens when you leave a pile of books in sight and they have a quick snoop around when you aren't there. As stated earlier, no teacher, irrespective of experience level, is ever up to date with their entire marking which is why snooping can pose potential problems if you underhandedly get caught. A snooper may 'grass you up' as sneakily as they looked at your books. To avoid being snooped, the rule is simple: if you haven't marked it, hide it, or at least don't leave it in an obviously accessible place. Don't, however, get paranoid. Most of your colleagues are as behind on their marking as you are, hence ipso facto most colleagues are not snoopers. But you always get that one colleague who is self-righteous, has no life, is desperate to get promoted (albeit wrongly) or is just plain malicious.

2.

The Don'ts of the School Email System

No doubt you have had training on the potential perils of social media. You may have also had general guidance on your school email system, for example emails are monitored, don't send each other jokes/forwards, be 'professional' and so on. But what about those little grey areas about which you are just unsure? Every school has its own email culture; a set of unwritten rules about emails. Generally speaking however, there are definite dos and don'ts with regard to how they should be written, what can and cannot go in them, who they are sent to and so on. When you read this chapter, it's up to you to decide whether a given rule fits into your own school's email culture. Please bear in mind however, that this guidance is ultimately designed for your defence, so if you follow it regardless of your school, you won't go wrong. This guidance predominantly applies when you are emailing more than one person, but can apply in other instances also. I'm sure you can distinguish.

Don't ramble

Be succinct, particularly when sending emails to many people. In addition to this, give them the option to delete it before they have read it. People hate having to read a long rambling email only to find out at the end that it does not affect them at all. Let's be honest, we hate reading emails. We find them a waste of time and they are literally the bane of people's lives in some schools, so don't write two paragraphs when two lines will do.

A typical email from a Head of Year 10 may read:

Assembly today

Could all year 10 teachers please bring their class to main hall for an assembly today at the start of period 2 as an outside speaker is coming in to talk about mental health. This will last no more than 35 minutes but it could be longer, we can never be certain. It depends on how quick the speaker gets through his material. Make sure all pupils and teachers go back to their normal period 2 lesson after. Make sure you accompany your pupils out of the hall as we do not want the chaos we had last time.

In itself, this is not long and is mostly clear. But when you have 20+ emails to read at 8:00am then the more succinct the better. It could be better simplified to:

If you are teaching year 10 period 2 today

Please bring your class to the main hall at the start of period 2. There will be an assembly about mental health.
Stay with them throughout the assembly, then go back to your normal period 2 lesson. Walk the pupils out.

It's short, to the point, and thanks to the clear header staff can delete it before reading it if it does not apply to them. Always bear in mind that while you may believe your email is more important than everyone else's, staff just want to read or delete them and get on with their lives as quickly as possible.

Don't use excessive punctuation

> Has anyone got the mark scheme for the C3 mock exam????????!!!!!!!!!!

If I received the email above, I would think the sender was anxious or panicked, and their negative emotions may transfer to me. Being somewhat stressed during term time as many teachers are, I definitely do not want this added to. I may even start to think that it was my job to get the mark scheme! Keep the emails plain. Don't be someone who creates a false sense of urgency as you risk making yourself unpopular; many people find this type of hyperbolic behaviour in emails annoying. If the above email had OFSTED!!!!!!! on it however, that would be more understandable!

Don't be sarcastic

Since the arrival of social media, the British are no longer allowed to be sarcastic. In a me-me-me world where people's feelings are ever more paramount, and a digital world that cannot easily recognise tone of voice, you run the risk of causing offence to a colleague and ending up in the Head's office. They will call you in and have a print out of your email on their desk ready while they rip you a new one (not a new email). A teacher I knew was once hauled into a Deputy Head's office for writing 'Take care, you sexy bitch!' on a close colleague's leaving card. The colleague knew it was being said in jest (and actually was amused) but the complaint came from another member of staff who simply assumed that said colleague would be offended. And this was just a card!

Don't use social media acronyms

Lol, lmao, xx, ;), ☺ and so on may all seem innocent and usually are, so you're probably wondering why on earth I am advising on such banality. The reason is simple: in schools, it's better to have an aura of professionalism, than the aura of somebody who just left university and spends most of their waking hours online. Using social media lingo (particularly when emailing many people) may give them the wrong impression. Also, like the sarcasm, these can be misconstrued. You may think it innocent to write 'xx' at the end of an email to an attractive NQT, but they might read into it differently. You might think 'lol' just means something made you smile, but the recipient may think they are being laughed at. It's also worth noting that emails, particularly those involving underachieving pupils, are often printed off and shown to external bodies and even parents. You don't want to appear unprofessional. Save the social media shorthand for social media.

Don't 'reply all' (if you can avoid it)

In my experience, and most probably yours too, when someone hits 'reply all' it's usually in response to a group email and there was an instruction they misunderstood, or there was essential information missing from the email.

For example, a Head of Year 7 sends the following email to all Year 7 Tutors:

Hi all,
Briefing today: 8:40am

Someone replies all:
Where is the briefing?

In most cases the Head of Year will 'reply all' right back with the location of the meeting. However, be aware of the fact that you have just highlighted their error publicly. There is a chance that they will be annoyed by this even though they may not express it to you. In general, any email you send that necessitates highlighting somebody's error, avoid the 'reply all' function.

Don't single out individual staff

If you're a middle leader you may want to highlight names of staff who have not done their reports on time, or whose results aren't in the system. You may want to praise the staff who showed good practice when you dropped in on them last week. As a general rule, you should neither praise nor condemn individuals in a group email. The condemned will feel resentment towards you, as will those who weren't praised. The praised may be happy they were identified, but the high will only last until it is crushed by the negativity of some jealous staff. In short, unless you are giving specific instructions to individuals and it is essential for other staff to know about it, avoid singling out individuals in emails. Also take care to avoid this directly or indirectly, for example by mentioning an underachieving group without mentioning the teacher by name; it's the same thing.

Don't send whole school emails (unless you have to)

Staff find lazy emails annoying. What do I mean by lazy emails? The kind that gets sent to the whole school without any rhyme or reason and it's obvious that the sender couldn't be bothered to send it only to the necessary staff. They didn't bother because this would involve them getting off their ass and actually knowing who it's relevant to, and finding out their email address. It was easier for them to just select the 'allstaff' mailing list. Don't let this be you. Firstly you will annoy colleagues by wasting their time, and secondly you won't even get your message across; staff delete 'all school' emails before any other and they will have a very good excuse of 'I didn't realise it was specifically for me' when they miss your information. Where possible avoid whole school emails, but it is understood that occasionally it's necessary.

Don't 'cc' people into emails (unless you have to)

This is the absolute worst of school email crimes and it can have a couple of different forms, both of which cause much annoyance to the recipient. Usually, you will receive an email about something which you have to do, or about something you have not done, and the person(s) cc'd in in both scenarios are leaders in some capacity. The purpose of the email then is either to force you to do something quickly – the person, in effect, is saying 'Do it now because the big guns are watching', or to show you up – 'You haven't done this, explain yourself to the big guns'. Ladies and gentleman, if you use cc in either of the aforementioned scenarios then you will make yourself very unpopular. You will be seen as a snitch, (those of you who teach in the inner city will know that snitches get stitches) or you'll actually undermine your own authority. Can you not be heard without threatening to set your leadership buddy on people? Or are you like the irritating little kid who can annoy people with impunity because they have a tough big brother? Staff who send such emails often argue that they are doing this not to snitch, but because so and so has to know that they've sent the necessary email. My response to this? Tough! Forward it to them afterwards. Unless certain people absolutely need to know the content of your email in real time do not cc them in. Given its high potential for causing a lot of annoyance, it's better to be overcautious for this one.

Don't incriminate yourself

Remember that emails are pretty much permanent. In any email, never write anything that could compromise your professionalism. Examples include insulting pupils to colleagues, complaining about decisions from the leadership team or backbiting other colleagues. There's no such thing as a throwaway comment on an email, so don't give people evidence with which to incriminate you.

And finally, take a deep breath

It is inevitable that at some stage, someone will rile you in an email. In the event of this inevitability, before you click reply, or, heaven forbid, 'reply all', take a deep breath.

Remember that if you are unprofessional in an email, whether or not you were acting in retaliation is irrelevant. You still risk a 'meeting' with a senior manager over your conduct. Take a deep breath. Then go and find the person who riled you and tell them exactly how you feel. Well, maybe not exactly.

A note about checking emails

First and foremost you are a teacher. Your job is to instil a love of learning and help your pupils achieve their full potential. Everything else is secondary. When you start your working day, do so with this in mind and never be held hostage by somebody else's schedule. While communication, particularly in large schools, is important, don't prioritise checking and responding to emails over your planning and marking – see Chapter 8 for more on why this is a bad idea. When you bump into your pupils in five or 10 years' time, they will be happy to see you because you taught them well, had a good sense of humour and perhaps most importantly because they had a good relationship with you. They will never thank you for checking your emails.

3.

How to Get Promoted and Other Things to Consider

You may be at the point in your career where you are considering taking on more responsibility. You may have applied for a TLR and were unsuccessful. You may be totally undecided on the direction of you career and whether to climb the ladder or not. Whatever your situation, this chapter should help you with your decision making.

How to Get Promoted

You've just found out that there's going to be a Head of Department, Head of Year, or some other juicy position up for grabs soon enough. You've decided it's right up your alley and you're going to go for it. Here's some advice for when you want that promotion:

Do the job before you get the job

You find out that someone is retiring soon and there will be a Head of xyz position coming up in a few months. A good plan of action would firstly be to express interest in the position to those that need to be aware. Following this, ask if you can shadow or help out the person currently in the position, during some of your free periods perhaps. In most schools they will be keen for you to get involved and will also be impressed by your proactivity. You will also benefit, as you will have detailed inside knowledge of the position before you've been appointed and will therefore stand out at the interview stage. Even if you are unsuccessful, the school will respect your drive and enthusiasm and will be more likely to consider you for future positions.

You must be positive at all times

If you want to get promoted, you cannot be the person that sits in the staffroom moaning for a living. Obviously we all need a bloody good moan from time to time, and I personally believe that not only is it healthy to do so, but also a key British value. However, once you have decided you want the promotion you have to stop, or, if you must moan, make sure your moans are more of a humorous release. Don't give the impression that you can't cope or that your workload is too much for you. Why would anyone give you more if you can't cope with the minimum?

You must show passion as well as ability

Simply caring about the kids (or claiming to) is not enough to get you promoted; a lack of wisdom cannot be compensated for with passion. When you're being interviewed for the post, make sure you show that you not only care about the kids, but that you have a plan to ensure the best for them. Bring an action plan with you to the interview stating a list of everything you will do in the first half term post-appointment. Make sure you are able to explain how you will implement, monitor and review your strategies.

You must be a 'yes' person

Yes, you read that correctly, but let me finish. While it's important that you do have your own ideas, methods, and strategies, the reality is that many of the ideas you are going to put into practice will not be your own. Because of this, argumentative or overly opinionated individuals can be seen as problematic. Show your laid-back compromising side while at the same time not completely letting go of your maverick tendencies. After all, they still want people who can lead and motivate others. Keep the balance.

People have to know you (and like you)

Throughout my career I have constantly heard the school environment being described as 'emotionally charged'. I'm sure this has many meanings, but the key thing to take from this is that in order for people to wholeheartedly follow you as a leader (not just half-assedly because they have to) they have to know you and like you. Rightly or wrongly, it is simply a fact: it will be difficult to lead your colleagues on any initiative if you sit in your room on your phone during break or don't join in the banter during lunch time. If you want a wider school role and colleagues in other departments don't know you, it will be harder for you to suddenly get them on board with your ideas. It's a good idea to raise your profile before going for that promotion and by no means do you have to be an extroverted person to accomplish this. Simple small talk goes a long way; when you see a colleague in passing, say 'Hello, how are you?' and so on. You may want to make an effort to go to your main staffroom and not just your departmental one during break time and do the same there. Unfortunately, with so many individuals leaving the profession, the sheer volume of supply teachers at many schools is enough for people to forget or not know people. Make the effort.

Are you an alpha?

A potential middle leader must have emotional strength, interpersonal skills, enthusiasm and the highest level of motivation in order to succeed. However, a major personality trait that makes for successful middle leadership is that of alphaness. Before you decide to take on additional responsibility, particularly middle leadership, you must have an honest discussion with yourself. Are you an alpha personality? Do your colleagues do as you do? Are you listened to or are you ignored? Are you cool and calm in a crisis or do you get panicked and flustered? Can you be friends with your colleagues and at the same time tell them that their marking is poor? Can you defend your department to an ever-scrutinising leadership team, or would you get tongue-tied? Do frequent changes and last minute deadlines bother you or can you take it all in stride? When a colleague does something to annoy you, do you deal with them one-to-one, or go bitching about them to everyone else? A middle leader can be like James Bond, Margaret Thatcher, a silverback gorilla, or anyone else you consider to be alpha. But what must be conveyed and genuinely believed is 'Whatever it is, I can deal with it'.

Now before you answer negatively to all of the previous questions and are put off middle leadership forever, remember that the characteristic of alphaness is helpful to you and your team, but not essential. You may have other skills and characteristics that may abrogate the need for alphaness, but life for you and your team will be much easier if you can comfortably say that you are an alpha.

If you follow this advice, usually somebody from the leadership team will approach you and say something to the effect of 'You know there's a Head of xyz position coming up? We really think you should go for it'. Good luck!

What am I letting myself in for? Is it for me?

You may be undecided on whether or not to go for a promotion. You may have seen many of your younger colleagues getting promoted ahead of you, and even though it bothers you, you just don't know if you want the extra work. Teaching a full timetable is hard enough so why on earth would you want more to stress about? But at the same time, you may feel subjugated because you are 'just' a teacher and you could really use the extra money. You may also like the idea of building a department from scratch, putting your own personal stamp on an initiative, or simply having more status at school. What should you do? The advice that follows should help you organise your thoughts.

All about the money?

You cannot do a TLR for the money alone. Let me save you the suspense by telling you that the money is not worth it, at least not for the smaller TLRs. You will be adding hours of additional work to your already busy week, and most schools will give very little time off from your timetable to do it in. Let me repeat – the money is not worth it for the smaller TLRs. Find something else to motivate you or just do some tuition on the weekends instead as it's less work, less stress and pays a lot more. On the other hand, a smaller TLR is usually a prerequisite to a larger TLR which makes more sense economically. You may begin with the former in order to do the latter, so you may want to take a smaller TLR as a stepping stone.

A deep sense of satisfaction

While it has been advised that the smaller TLRs don't make economical sense, this doesn't mean that you should dive right in because the larger TLRs do. In addition to the characteristics described, for you to do justice to the role, yourself and ultimately the kids, there has to be a deep sense of satisfaction derived from the responsibility undertaken. In teaching, it is rare that the money compensates the blood, sweat and tears. Remember, there's no rule that says you have to climb the career ladder. If your heart's not in it, don't do it.

Stuck in the middle

The main source of complaint from larger TLR holders such as Heads of Department or Heads of House/Year, is that their teaching suffers because of TLR responsibilities. There simply aren't enough hours in the day to keep up with both responsibilities to the best of your ability. If you are a perfectionist then staying in the classroom might be the better option, or you may have to change your outlook and accept that you will have to become an expert in prioritising and even missing out the less important things. Be aware that the most stress in the school organisation is in the middle. One of my former Heads of Department put it bluntly when he said 'you get shit from above and below'. Those above you and below you will expect perfection (which you will try to deliver but won't be able to) and they don't always show empathy or sympathy when getting anything less. If you have not mastered your workload as a teacher, it would be risky for you to go for a larger TLR and it would be advisable to wait a couple of years, perhaps after you've done a smaller TLR as a stepping stone.

On the other hand, after you have considered these factors, believe in yourself and take on the role wholeheartedly, as this is key. While it is necessary to make an informed decision, you must not be in a negative or fearful frame of mind once you have made your decision.

4.

When and How to Say No and Yes

Keenness and enthusiasm are double-edged swords in teaching. These qualities, which can allow you to climb the grease pole with ease, are the same qualities that can cause you unbearable stress and, in the worst cases, push you right out of the profession. Schools have almost no limit in what they will try and get their staff to do. The reality is that once something is done 'for the children' it becomes insignificant how many adults have their need for a life-work balance compromised. It is important that you look after yourself and be careful what you agree to do or not do. This chapter aims to outline the issues surrounding saying 'yes' or 'no'.

You love the praise

You can get a reputation quite quickly as a yes-person. Many young staff love the praise they initially receive from their superiors for always volunteering to do x or help out with y. However, the high they get from the praise soon dies and within a couple of years, all they have left is resentment. You may be keen and enthusiastic and that is good, but you are nobody's pet donkey: it's not your job to take on an extra responsibility (which you don't really want) for free, and it is not your job to do the things that more experienced colleagues are outright refusing. Be calculated and measured in what you agree to do or you will have regrets in the long run.

Before you say yes

Before you say yes, you may want to ask yourself a few important questions: Will this improve my teaching/results of my pupils? Will this raise my profile with the pupils? Is this something that will help me be considered for promotion? Will the leadership team find out about me taking this initiative? How much time will this take? Is everyone else doing this? How bad will it look if I refuse? Think first!

Having said this, it is advisable that you do say 'yes' when it's in your interests to do so, especially if you are in a school where a particular task is the norm. By saying no when everyone else is saying yes, you run the risk of becoming a magnet for school bullies – see Chapter 9 for more on this.

Be calculated and measured. Neither yes nor no should be your kneejerk response, but every yes should be reserved for the things that matter to you. Your relationships and physical and mental health however will suffer if you are a yes-person.

How They Get You to Say Yes and What to Do About It

During a half term trash TV binge, I can remember watching a documentary on pimps and pimping. A gold-toothed, fur-coat-wearing, limo-driving pimp stereotype said that the word 'pimp' is an acronym: Person In Manipulative Power or P.I.M.P. This description can also apply to some school leaders: some school leaders are P.I.M.Ps. They will try and get you to do things (beyond your teaching load) that you don't want to, often but not always through some form of manipulation. As I am still in the profession, and I'd like to remain so, I'd like to insert a disclaimer: this comparison is tongue in cheek and deliberately outrageous for the sake of humour! The tactics P.I.M.Ps use and how to deal with them can be best illustrated in the following examples – but bear in mind these are by no means exhaustive.

Flattery

At a certain school there was a TLR available for a particular responsibility in the history department. The staff were fully aware of the bureaucracy involved in this role and did not want anything to do with it. Nobody applied. The Head of Department approached one member of staff and said something to the effect of 'The Headteacher has seen your level of dedication to the kids, and we think you should consider the TLR. It would be perfect for you. The leadership team and the kids think you're amazing. It would be good for you if you stretched yourself and progressed your career'.

The member of staff then considered applying for the TLR as his ego was well satiated. At the pub the following week, he spoke to his colleagues and almost all of them were given the exact same sales pitch by the exact same person! They all had a good laugh and stuck to their guns. The lesson here? Don't be fooled: if you are suddenly being showered with compliments and there is some donkey work that needs doing, it is unlikely to be a coincidence.

Duping

A teacher was approached in the corridor at break time and asked if they wanted to go on a trip to Poland with 10 high ability pupils over half term. They were given an outline of the itinerary of the trip, which seemed appealing, and the paperwork for the trip was already complete. The teacher agreed. When the teacher returned from Poland, they were asked to write a full report on the impact of the trip and present it to governors. The lesson here? Find out everything before agreeing to anything. This teacher was duped as they were pushed to make a quick decision (in the corridor) and they were not given the full information. If you are not confident enough to ask 21 questions to those above you, then a simple 'Sorry, I'm really busy the moment. Would you be able to put that in an email and I'll let you know?' will suffice. That way, at least if later you are tricked into doing something you will have solid grounds to refuse.

Coercion: everyone's doing it so you have to

At one school, there was increasing pressure to come in on a Saturday morning to do paid revision sessions. Most of the established staff valued their Saturday morning over the moneys received for revision sessions and so were reluctant to attend. A Head of Department, who was keen to prove himself to the leadership team, would approach the not-so-keen staff while they were alone, and tell them that lots of other staff had now signed up for a Saturday session and that they were one of only a couple who hadn't. He would have a clipboard ready along with a pen and ask which Saturday they wanted to do. He would then casually slip in (with a disappointed look) that they didn't have to do the sessions, but pupils wouldn't revise of their own accord and performance management would look at all areas of provision for pupils. Being alone meant that the member of staff would struggle to find out if they were being told the truth about other staff, and also made it impossible to have backup from fellow colleagues who didn't want to attend either. Naturally, the teacher felt coerced and was deliberately made to feel so. In this case, a simple 'I have a wedding coming up but I can't remember which Saturday. Can I get back to you?' would suffice. At least then you'll have time to think or consult. The fake wedding excuse works for anything involving weekends. If you are later asked 'How was the wedding?' just recall and give details of an actual wedding you have attended in the past. If you feel guilty about lying, remember that you aren't obliged to work on weekends; therefore lying about how you spent your own time is justifiable as it is nobody's business in the first instance!

Not-so-subtle subtlety

In another school, two open days were planned and it was decided by the Headteacher that these would take place on two different Saturday mornings of the school year. The Headteacher announced during briefing that he respected his staff's need for a work-life balance, and said 'We do not expect all staff to attend both mornings'. Can you see how he subtly obliged his staff to at least one Saturday morning, even though strictly speaking he couldn't as the school still followed the School Teachers' Pay and Conditions Document (STPCD)? Read between the lines.

How to Say No Without Saying No

Useful 'no' phrases

Many P.I.M.Ps will not use the aforementioned tactics and will instead outright ask you to do something that you don't want to. The same way that saying 'I don't know' in industry is career suicide, saying 'no' in teaching can be just as dangerous if you don't have the correct finesse described in this chapter. Get to grips with some easy to use 'no' phrases:

'I can't on that day. I have a wedding/christening/appointment to go to'

'I'm really busy with my top set year 11 at the moment, so now is probably not the best time. I'm spending all of my energy on getting them through their mock exams'

'I'm unsure at the moment. Can you put it in an email and I'll get back to you once I get a chance to think? I've had such a busy week'

In each of the above, you are saying no by referring to circumstances out of your control, or the reasons given are mainly professional ones. Just make sure you sound believable and your tone of voice should convey that you would love to do said task if only you were able.

Keep your mouth shut: saying no by not saying anything

Be careful what you are good at, or tell people you are good at. Yes, you read that correctly. Allow me to explain: a school that is managed correctly (stop chuckling) will delegate staff according to their strengths. Remember that schools will act in the interests of their pupils well before the interests of staff, and this has the potential to cause some bother. This can best be illustrated through a handful of examples:

- A Deputy Head sent an email asking for people to be put on the first aid rota. Ms Khan knew first aid and casually mentioned this in a conversation with another colleague. She did not, however, want the responsibility of being on the first aid rota. The rota didn't get filled with volunteers and word got round that Ms Khan knew first aid. The Deputy Head approached her directly and 'asked' if she wanted to be on the rota. She didn't have the confidence to say no and so ended up on the rota.

- A science teacher mentioned in passing that he had an LGV license. A PE teacher was off with a long-term illness so the science teacher was 'asked' to take the football team to away games. He did not want to do this. But he did.

- A maths teacher of Afghani descent was fluent in Pashtun. He was 'asked' to translate every now and again at meetings with parents. He did not want to do this. But he did. And to add insult to injury, it wasn't until 8 months later that he found out he should have been paid for it.

If you have a skill and you fear a school may take advantage of you for it, keep your mouth shut. Unless of course you are happy to use your skill in the directed way, in which case, don't lose sight of your key professional duties: no number of favours will compensate poor teaching.

Too Negative?

People outside of the teaching profession, and indeed some ignorant people within, may be taken aback by this chapter and accuse the author of encouraging laziness, or even a disregard for pupils. Hopefully this last section will allay your fears. One of the aims of this book is to keep teachers from losing their enthusiasm by fostering a work-smart ethic which focuses on the bread and butter of teaching without building resentment: this inevitably involves saying 'no' to the mundane, the extraneous, and the unbearable.

Take the initiative

Saying 'no' to a superior can be awkward and nerve-wracking, particularly for newer teachers. To make it easier to say no, it is helpful if you are already showing initiative elsewhere. For example, Mr Bloggs runs a very popular after school science club for an hour a week as he is passionate about science and wants his pupils to achieve and have fun; a noble and productive use of his time. He was asked to come into school for an open day on a Saturday. It was easy for him to refuse the open day by saying 'I can't this week. Science club is going to be running over time as we're doing xyz and I've got loads of marking to do as well'. Mr Bloggs is clearly a keen member of staff and his dedication will be known as he is already engaging and enthusing pupils in his own time without any compulsion: he is free from the burden of open day. In fact, if Mr Bloggs was ever under extreme pressure to do more, he could always use his science club as a bargaining chip: he could just cancel it citing additional workload as a reason, thereby making the school think twice. The conclusion from this is that you will feel a lot better about saying no, and will be in a stronger position to do so, if you know that your school both needs you and wants you. By adapting an attitude similar to Mr Bloggs you can be in control of your career and not a victim of it. As Machiavelli once said (not that I know anything about him other than this): control or be controlled. Be a committed teacher, but go above and beyond in the things that you enjoy doing rather than being a slave to the things you don't. This will ensure the wellbeing of you and your pupils.

5.

The Dos and Don'ts of Meetings

You've just finished a long hard teaching day and were looking forward to a cup of coffee before you start your planning for tomorrow. You turn the page of your planner and there it is, in big clear letters that dreaded word: Meeting.

Let's just put it out there in the open and stop dancing around the issue: we all hate meetings. We have too many other things we could be getting on with, and we don't want to sit there listening to somebody telling us something in an hour which could probably have taken five minutes if we could be bothered to concentrate.

This chapter contains advice for both the attendees and the chair. If you want the meeting process to be a lot more bearable, then take heed.

Attendees

Don't prolong the meeting

Don't keep putting your hand up to ask questions, and don't argue over irrelevant details. If a meeting overruns by 15 minutes because you think KS3 should have red exercise books and KS4 should have blue, then expect there to be a dartboard with a picture of your face on it in the staffroom the next day. Just receive the information and get out of there. Save your energy (and everybody else's patience) for the things that matter. Meetings often get unnecessarily prolonged when individual staff insist on being overly opinionated over triviality, or when they argue against decisions which have already been made. If you are not happy with a new change, idea, etc. and you are fully aware the decision was not made by anyone present at the meeting, then don't prolong the meeting by overly expressing your concerns, your confusion, your agitation or other misgivings. Departmental, house, pastoral or year group meetings are not the forum for trying to get decisions reversed. Save it for the union meetings. This does not apply however, if you have actually been asked to be involved in the decision-making process in that particular meeting.

Don't moan

As mentioned previously, some moaning is essential and I believe it is also necessary to keep a teacher's sanity. In addition to this, what a teacher does at break time and lunchtime (providing it's legal!) is nobody's business. This is one of the reasons Ofsted are disallowed from entering the staffroom as it is purely the domain of the staff: in teacher territory, moan away! But do take this with a pinch of salt as if you get a reputation for it, your leadership team will be most unimpressed. Moaning at a departmental meeting, however, will do you no favours. You will waste the time and energy of staff with your negativity (or perceived negativity) and even more importantly, it will make you look a weaker teacher in the eyes of your superiors. Your Head of Department may not comment, and they may even attempt to diffuse your moaning through humour, but they will be making silent judgements. Try not to appear as if you can't cope. However, if you do have a genuine concern and the meeting allows you to express this then do so unemotionally using logic and evidence to back up your points. For example 'The new curriculum is way too hard-there is no way in hell my year 10s are going to achieve their target grades. It's ridiculous!' could be much better expressed as 'The new curriculum has got a lot of the old A-level in. I think all year 10 teachers should discuss how to teach key topics otherwise we risk them not getting their target grades'

In essence, both statements are making the same point, but can you see how the latter is more solution-based than problem-based? Save the moaning for the union meetings.

Show initiative

As we have already established, you do not want to be there, but since you have no choice, it's in your professional interest to show initiative. Turn up on time, not five minutes late with a coffee mug in your hand, have your note pad ready and note down key points, and don't talk when the chair is talking. Keep your eyes on the speaker and don't drift off, be sociable but don't socialise, use humour but don't overdo it, ask intelligent questions and seek clarification. Saying nothing at all may indicate indifference. If there are refreshments, don't treat them a like a buffet! Don't be sarcastic or mock the ideas of others and don't be argumentative. Remember, at a meeting you are on display so you should endeavour to look your best.

Advice for Chairs

Be organised

Teachers know all too well that some meetings are just 'fillers': there is a meeting calendared and middle leaders cannot think of anything that needs doing, so they lamely and obviously give some mundane or disorganised task to keep you annoyingly busy for an hour. If you are a middle leader/chair of meetings, please stop doing this! Your staff will be much more motivated if you send them the agenda the night before, tell them the purpose of a task and give them very specific instructions. Don't send an email the night before saying 'Hi all there is a meeting calendared for tomorrow. Can we use the time to update schemes of work? Thank you'. Which schemes of work? What does update mean? You simply cannot expect staff do this properly. If you don't care, your staff won't either. Be organised.

Bring refreshments

These are important. You catch more flies with honey than you do with vinegar. Show your team you value them. Refreshments can go a long way, and your staff are more than likely going to be very tired so give them a boost!

Be succinct

Don't allow the meeting to go off on a tangent and therefore become unnecessarily prolonged. Use humour to diffuse any disruption, moaning, etc. from staff if you know it is unnecessary and detracting from the purpose of the meeting. Also people, especially teachers, are not good at sitting and listening for prolonged periods of time, so don't make them! Get staff involved, give them things to do, ask for opinions and so on.

Be polite

Never scourge individual staff in a meeting. If you are a middle leader you no doubt will be sick of some staff just not doing as they're told, but a meeting is not the time to blow your top. Your team will lose respect for you and you will lose their trust by demonstrating a lack of emotional self-control. They will fear that they are next in your line of fire.

6.

How to Get Parents on Your Side

As a teacher, you will encounter many different types of parent and an entire book could be written solely on parents and parenting. From narcissistic mothers who couldn't care less about their daughter's underachievement, but will spend fifteen minutes telling you that everyone thinks they are sisters, to hyper-ambitious fathers who will settle for nothing less than their son becoming a heart surgeon by the end of next term. You will meet them all. Our job as teachers is to get parents on board with our objective: for our pupils to achieve their full potential. In light of this, there are three main types of parent we need be aware of, and we need to know how best to get them on side. This list is by no means exhaustive, and individual experiences will vary, however if you work at a middle of the range comprehensive school, which most schools are, the advice that follows will help you with achieving your objective.

The Aspirational Parent

This type of parent has a very intelligent child, and is keen for their child to maintain their high standards. There is a good chance you like the child as their behaviour is immaculate and they have a maturity that you find refreshing. You may even wonder why on earth these parents even bother coming to parents' evening as they already seem to know how good their child is. When speaking with parents like this, it is important to know (and as hard as it may be to believe) that these parents did not make an appointment with you just to get their ego massaged. When giving feedback, make sure it's specific. A general 'She's doing really well' just won't cut it. These parents want to know specific areas in which their child can improve, and how. Be ready with the well-deserved praise, but also have some recommendations for revision guides, and harder topics in which she could have done even better if she were to xyz.

Unseen Parents

Once upon a time, I was an NQT looking forward to parents' evening so I could speak to the parents of all of my misbehaved pupils and gleefully watch while they got read the riot act. Sadly, my fantasy didn't come to fruition. The parents did not attend parents' evening, and even the Heads of House struggled to get them to come into school. If they did, they were sometimes aggressive and often accused the school of victimisation.

Unfortunately, you will simply not see the parents/guardians of pupils whom you will want to see the most. In the event that you do come across the parent of a pupil who has extreme behaviour issues, or is very disengaged from education, it is important that you say it as it is. Many new(ish) teachers shy away from being direct with parents as they fear that it makes them look weak, or fear that the parent might be rude to them, or they simply see it as a confrontation that they would rather not have. When dealing with such a parent, it is important that you are focused on solutions rather than problems, and on building positive relationships rather than punishments. When reading this section you may even be thinking of a particular pupil and it's almost certainly the case that sanctions don't really have the desired effect of improving their behaviour.

When giving your concerns about a pupil to their parent/guardian, do so unemotionally. It's better to sound more like a news reporter than a guest on a daytime talk show. Let them know the child's issues, but at the same time make it obvious that you can see some good in their child and are willing to work with this – without compromising your boundaries of course. For example:

'Johnny is constantly disrupting the lesson by shouting out and making noises and I have to keep sending him out. Not a single lesson has been taught without disruption from Johnny. Both myself and the other kids are getting very annoyed.'

Could be better phrased as:

'Johnny has so much potential but it's a shame he wastes it when he's disrupting lessons. It's such a shame that he has to be repeatedly removed from the lesson because he inhibits his own learning and that of others. If Johnny chose to channel his energy more carefully, he would be a high achieving pupil and a credit to the class. If the misbehaviour continues then I'm afraid I have no choice but to keep sending him out. It would be a real shame if Johnny does not achieve what he is so very clearly capable of.'

The parent will more than likely respond better to the second statement than the first. The added bonus for those teachers who may fear a confrontation is that the second statement is not only much easier to hear, but also much easier to say. If however you are in a situation where the parent is being unreasonably confrontational or verbally abusive, just walk away. A simple 'I'm sorry but I'm not going to be spoken to like that' is sufficient. Then report the parent to your leadership team. You are perfectly within your rights by avoiding being verbally abused, and also, if you stick around, you risk the consequences of retaliatory abuse, particularly if you are hot-tempered. Just walk away. It's easier.

The Average Parent

Most of the parents you deal with genuinely want the best for their kids. They want them to do their best in their exams, and to be well behaved. They want them to leave school with good career prospects and to be respected by their peers and their teachers. So what then you ask, is the problem?

An article a few years ago stated that the long-hours culture of many jobs is leaving parents without the emotional energy to engage with their kids.[1] Another article stated that it is common (and detrimental) for parents to make their child their friend or confidante.[2] The point? The average parent will want all of the aforementioned successes, but will not, perhaps due to some combination of the reasons described, follow the necessary steps to achieve or enforce them. Please note that I am not a parent and so this is at best an attempt to explain my personal experiences.

Here's an example: A teacher meets a parent at parents' evening and complains that Steve is repeatedly taking out his phone in class and that this is causing disruption in the lesson. The parent agrees and gives Steve a scathing look and tells him not to do it again. The teacher believes that the point has been made and that his lessons will henceforth be phone free. But guess what happens two days later? The parent and teacher in this scenario believed that the words were enough: they weren't. You will come across many parents who, for whatever reason, do not enforce the behaviour or attitude that they desire from their child. While it is not our job to teach parenting to parents, it is our job to get parents on side and keep them there. This is where you can make a huge impact just by learning a couple of small gems.

When hearing the parent tell Steve off for using his phone in class, the teacher could have taken the opportunity to encourage the parent to enforce a sanction. They could have said any of the following statements:

'How are we going to make sure he keeps it away?'

Notice the use of 'we' emphasising that both teacher and parent are working together. Notice also the open-ended question intended to invite the parent to think of, and hence enforce, a sanction.

'Can I make a suggestion?'

Sometimes parents just won't suggest a sanction no matter how much you hint at it. In this case, just ask the question above. A parent will never say no, and as you asked you're merely suggesting and not imposing. When they do say yes, suggest a punishment you deem reasonable, for example confiscating Steve's phone for a week. The parent may not follow through with it, but you've at least got them thinking and you really never know! It will often be the case that the average parent will be hesitant to carry out a sanction or removal of a privilege for long periods of time as their kids will nag them and the average parent struggles to resist. In light of this, it is important that you begin with a smaller sanction and make sure the punishment matches the crime.

It's a good idea to use the threat of telling parents about the behaviour or attitude of pupils, purely to see how the pupil responds. Often the pupil will try and save face by saying 'I don't care, tell them'. When you do come to tell the parent, make sure you tell them that too. The parent is far more likely to issue and follow through with a sanction when they feel their own authority has been undermined.

For the sake of the example, only the use and enforcement of sanctions has been mentioned. There is no reason, however, why a teacher may not invite parents to encourage their child through rewards. Be careful though. Suggesting an expensive reward may make the parent feel uncomfortable. You may want to leave the rewarding to them after merely suggesting it as a possible motivator. The focus on solutions and relationship building when dealing with the average parent is not amiss, and every type of parent should be approached in the spirit of positivity and with a clear emphasis on the best interests of the child.

7.

Guidance for Trainee Teachers

You've heard the horror stories, the inspiring stories and you have even observed teachers before you decided to embark on the journey. You may have wanted to work with kids your whole life, or you may even just be a graduate looking for your first job and you know there's a demand for teachers in particular subjects. Whatever your situation, you've decided to take the plunge and you're about to begin your training. This chapter should help you do your best and get the most out of it.

Be aware, I have decided not to beat around the bush or soften the truth, as I am certain that anything less than absolute honesty is of no benefit to a potential teacher. Consider this tough love: I am toughening you up by keeping you informed and advised, even if it you don't quite like it!

Essential Information for Potential Trainee Teachers

Before you embark on the journey of teacher training, read, digest and even memorise the next two subsections:

The myth

'You teachers have got it easy. Work six hours a day with long holidays. Nice and cushy!'

You will have heard many different versions of the above statement, perhaps from your non-teacher friends or just in passing. This myth has also been perpetuated by some elements of popular media. Before you read any further, fully detox yourself from this myth. Rid yourself of it in its entirety, as there is not a nuance of truth in it. If there is any part of you that disagrees with me, thinks that I'm exaggerating, or that teachers just like moaning, or anything else that gives the myth credibility, then save yourself the bother and choose another career now while it's still easy to do so. There is no burden on the author to prove the fallacy of the myth in this section as it is evident from the entire book.

You're not at uni any more

If you don't realise this early you are doomed. Your university days are now over. Irrespective of your training route, it is important that you realise that teacher training is not like your undergraduate degree. You cannot, and indeed will not, be able to go out drinking three times a week, stay up late, survive on minimal sleep or complete assignments last minute, and you will also struggle to make full weekend plans. You will be working every evening, except for probably Friday (because you will be too tired) and one day on the weekend also. There is no way around this and you have to accept that some aspects of your life will have to be put on hold. If you are in the middle of pursuing some other goal or major interest which you cannot give up or cut down, then it would be best for you to defer your training until a more suitable time.

Now that you have had the reality check and still want to become a teacher, it is essential for you to be aware of the qualities and characteristics necessary for teaching. When reading these, remember that everyone has all of these qualities, albeit in varying capacities, and that they can be developed.

Emotional strength

Teaching is going to test every part of your character, your mind, body, and whatever else you can imagine. A trainee teacher was overweight and this made her somewhat self-conscious. On her first lesson with her first class, a pupil said to her 'Miss have you always been so fat or did you have to eat loads?' – the poor lady was in tears and never returned. Are you like this teacher? If so, then teaching is not for you! In dealing with this type of situation, you must have either a very good sense of humour, or have emotional strength that matches the physical strength of Dwayne 'The Rock' Johnson. The previous example is actually somewhat tame. Most teachers can and do ignore abusive behaviour from pupils, however it is a lot more difficult to ignore adults. While your mentors and other teachers are not going to abuse you per se, they are going to scrutinise you quite heavily and you will feel like it's personal. You will have criticisms, or should I say areas for development, such as, 'The pupils were bored by your monotonous voice', 'You don't smile enough', 'The kids see you as arrogant, 'You aren't being assertive enough' or 'You haven't built a positive relationship with the class' and so on. The list is endless. Get into the right frame of mind before you start. Tell yourself 'I can take this and I will learn from it'. Repeat that in your mind three times before feedback from every lesson (if you indeed decide to go ahead with teacher training).

Stage presence

If ever there was a 'skill' needed for teaching, this is it. You will have to be objective when deciding whether or not you have this. Ask yourself the following questions and answer honestly:

Are you lively or mundane? Do you like talking to people or would you rather listen? Do people enjoy talking to you, or do you bore them? How do strangers respond to you? Do they meet you and forget you, or do they seem happy to see you the second time? Do you have an engaging tone of voice, or a plain monotonous delivery? Do people notice you or are you mostly in the background?

You can probably guess how you would ideally answer these questions if you are to have the stage presence necessary to be teacher. This section does however, come with a health warning lest the reader take offense: positive answers to the previous questions are merely good indicators of stage presence; they are not absolutes. There are many teachers who during social interactions would answer most of those questions in the negative, but in the classroom they are very good actors. You either have to have stage presence, or you have to act like you do. But it is easier if you are not acting.

Caring

Are you in it because you care? Do you genuinely want to see your pupils reach their full potential? Does the thought of pupils coming back and visiting you to thank you several years later make you smile, or are you indifferent? If you have a genuine interest in your pupils' achievement, wellbeing, or position in the world, then you're off to a good start. Being caring is a bit like stage presence: faking it until you make it will only get you so far. Teachers who are intrinsically motivated are better, stay in the profession longer, and have more resilience when it comes to dealing with the many adversities that come with a teaching career. You may not have thought about this concept in so much detail as of yet, but not to worry, your mind set is determined by you – in other words you can care if you choose to. So care! It will make it easier for you in the long run.

Organisation

Make no mistake, a teacher's workload is high, and a trainee teacher's workload is even higher. As said earlier, doing things last minute is impossible and the toll for being disorganised is a heavy one: you risk embarrassing yourself in front of your class through ill-preparedness, and the angry teacher watching your poorly planned lesson go to pot is not always going to be empathetic. You know those really annoying people that make to-do lists, stick post-it notes everywhere, save things in case they may need them and have everything and anything to hand when you ask them for it? Become one of them. There is more about this in Chapter 8.

Essential Information for Trainee Teachers

Now you have decided that you have the aforementioned qualities and characteristics, or can at least develop them, here is some advice for when you actually begin your teaching training:

Get off the phone

Let me reiterate: your uni days are over. When you are in the school environment, judgements will be made from the word go. What then are the implications of this? You must be professional at all times, not just when you're teaching. It will be frowned upon, even if it is not explicitly stated, if you are constantly on your phone when you should be planning lessons. And no one cares about your new tattoo, and they certainly don't want to know whom you woke up next to after a heavy weekend. You may see other teachers being less professional than you, and it can be tempting to join in. It is important that you remember that you are the trainee, not them, and unfortunately you have double standards to live up to. Your professionalism, dedication and enthusiasm are being judged (and privately discussed) even when you're not in the classroom. While it is important to balance these qualities with being human, try to keep the pendulum swinging more towards professionalism than, well... humanism. Steer conversations towards finding out how to improve your practice, not only in terms of lesson plans, but also in terms of parents' evenings, marking, trips and so on. Teachers love to talk; ask them questions then shut up and listen.

Do as you're told

Seem simple? Then why do so many trainees not do so?! Here's an example: Mr Bloggs' lesson was observed by the teacher whose class it was. The lesson was ok(ish) and the teacher gave Mr Bloggs three things to do, or at least try to do, in his next lesson. He told him to be more assertive and use the school behaviour policy to deal with any misbehaviour; to add pictures to his PowerPoint to make it more engaging; and to use past exam questions to assess progress. How many of these things do you think Mr Bloggs did? Wait for it... none. When the teacher called him on it during the feedback, Mr Bloggs said, 'I didn't realise I had to'. Dear trainees, when a qualified teacher suggests, advises, or something other than outright tells you to do something in your lesson, they are in fact telling you to do something in your lesson! Don't take advice or suggestions as literally that. You will have to show that you do in fact *take* advice and follow suggestions, hence you are better off viewing these as non-negotiable instructions. It is easier that way.

Don't argue

You're not qualified yet so don't argue. Here's an example: Ms Smith was given feedback for her lesson, which was not so good. She was told that for the class in question, short snappy activities would be better as the pupils were losing concentration with Ms Smith's university-style lecturing from the front. To the experienced teacher, it was self-evident that it was the poor teaching that led to disengaged pupils. Ms Smith however, insisted that she did no wrong. She argued that the pupils weren't listening to her because she was only a trainee, and that her lecture was interesting and fun and there was no possible way it would cause pupils to switch off. She claimed her style of teaching was different to that of the advising teacher, and she shouldn't have to be the same as her. The teacher now felt like she was being pressured to be less diplomatic and became somewhat irate, then insisted on her original point. Ms Smith became teary and walked away. In this example it is clear that Ms Smith was either becoming defensive, as she genuinely thought her lecture was a good one, or she was misinformed of the nature of teaching: the way you teach is highly regulated, and if pupils don't listen to you, it is considered to be your fault, not theirs. Either way, her arguing proved futile and only served to perturb her professionalism. Try not to get defensive and argue. If however you do feel you are being wrongly annihilated, a simple 'Have I done anything right this lesson?' should do the trick.

Don't undermine the teacher

During your practice, you will have to observe other teachers and most likely take over their classes. While observing you may see established teachers not quite teaching properly; you may see pupils off task, books unmarked and so on. It is important that you never negatively comment on the practice of another teacher. This is a guaranteed way of getting yourself into trouble, as if you undermine the person who is grading your lessons, they are less likely to give you the support which you will definitely need, or they may perceive you as arrogant and thus observe your lessons with even greater scrutiny. Remember that many teachers, even those with years of experience, are very sensitive to criticism and the last person they need it from is a trainee. If in doubt, just stay quiet.

You're not paranoid; they really are talking about you

As a trainee teacher you are constantly being monitored, often by many other teachers. Teachers will often bump into each other and have a natter about how you're getting on. They may even suddenly stop their conversation when they see you walking past. You will be a significant topic of discussion while you are on your placement and 99% of the discussion will take place behind your back. Get over it. Just make sure you are giving them something positive to talk about!

Always be respectful

A good teacher always has some degree of an emotional bond to their classes, even the ones they may not get on with so much. In light of this, and you will not like how this sounds, there is a very high probability that the teacher likes their class more than they like you: you're new and you're going to leave. The teacher may have taught the class for years. It is therefore important that you are always respectful towards the pupils. You may think this is obvious, but many trainee teachers (understandably so) struggle to keep their cool when a class is winding them up. While it is essential to maintain good discipline, you must do so respectfully or you will lose that from both the class and the teacher.

8.

Ensuring a Life-Work Balance

It is no secret that teachers are leaving the profession in droves, with most of them citing a poor work-life balance as the reason. A recent news article stated that 4 in 10 new teachers quit within a year of teaching,[3] and a further 50% plan to leave the profession within two years.[4] This data does not exactly fill a young teacher with joy, but it is of no use to anyone if we ignore the fact that many teachers, younger and older, simply reach breaking point and decide that enough is enough. The purpose of this chapter is not to appoint blame. The workload for teachers has been high for as long as I can remember and the reasons for this could fill an entire book. This chapter is not about changing the system, but about succeeding in the given system and concurrently retaining your wellbeing.

Leave your laptop at work

Unions report that teachers (without additional responsibility) work an average of 55 hours a week.[5] One of the positive aspects of our profession is that we can choose when it is we decide to do this work. I have met teachers who don't overdo it in the week, but compensate for this on weekends. I've met teachers who work from 8-11pm every night, and I have met teachers who come into school very early and leave late, hence avoiding taking any work home at all. How and when you work will depend on the variables in your life. It may be impossible for you to leave late if you have children to pick up from nursery or an elderly relative to care for, for example.

I personally, and I'm sure psychologists agree, favour the 'leave work at work' method. If it is possible for you, try the following work schedule, taking the normal breaks throughout the school day:

7:30am – Arrive at work

3:00-3:40pm – Have a break

6:00-6:30pm – Leave work, and leave your laptop at work

You may struggle to follow this schedule initially, as the last thing you want to do is continue working for another few hours after a long day teaching! In the long run however, you will find yourself much more relaxed when at home: you will have physically and mentally separated your work life from your home life.

Many teachers who leave school at around 4:30pm and continue working again at around 8:00pm, are plagued by a sense of urgency during the hours that they are not working, and they are not able to switch off and relax. As a result of this, they often feel like they have worked a 14 hour day rather than an 11 hour day, because they haven't actually had any downtime. In the long run, the cortisol levels in their blood will rise and this will lead to stress, which not only is counterproductive to their work performance, but also increases the risk of a wide range of health problems, including cardiovascular disease, weight gain and depression.[6] It is essential to appreciate however, that individual lifestyles and schedules vary, so it is impossible for everybody to attempt the above. However if you are able to, do it: come in early, stay late, and leave your laptop at school. As for the weekend? You only really have two options: you either leave around 6pm on Friday, or you work a few hours on Sunday. Friday is better as it would mean a totally free weekend. You decide.

Cut the crap

As a teacher, you are working around 10-15 hours more each week during term time than your non-teacher counterparts. This means that time for your hobbies, kids, gym and so on is limited. You can however increase the time left for yourself if you cut the crap:

Stop the household chores

Unless you really enjoy these, try and decrease them where possible. Get yourself a dishwasher; have your clothes ironed by a reasonably priced ironing service; cook in bulk at the weekend.

Switch to online grocery shopping

Some stores offer very cheap delivery options and it will save you hours each week.

Exercise at work

Does your school have a gym for staff? Even if it doesn't, know that some of the best exercises only require 30 minutes and an exercise mat. You could do these in your classroom before leaving so that when you are home you are totally relaxed. You might not want the caretakers to see you in your workout clothes, trying to do a press-up, but you will save hours a week in travelling time and you'll feel better because of it.

Find a gym near work

If working out at school is out of the question for you, join a gym near school or home, even if it's missing some of the mod cons. Do you want to save time or waste 20 minutes in traffic so you can sit in a sauna for a bit? The nearer it is to home or school the more often you can go, and the more time you will have for other things that matter to you.

Take up running

Being outdoors is proven to release serotonin, a hormone that counteracts stress.[7] So in addition to releasing the usual endorphins from exercise, which also counteract stress, your brain will release even more serotonin from being outdoors. An added bonus is that running is time efficient: you just run. No travelling time at all, thereby cutting the crap.

Stop lounging

Having a lie in can be comforting and indeed necessary, but lying in bed for two hours longer than necessary while you aimlessly play with your smartphone will serve no benefit to your work-life balance. You can maximise the time spent doing things that you truly desire to do by minimising the time spent on things which you are doing while on autopilot. Be efficient with your time.

Just as in the previous section, it is essential to note that individual schedules and lifestyles vary, so you may not be able to make all of these adjustments. But if you are easily able to sacrifice the mundane for the exciting, then why wouldn't you? Get off of autopilot today.

Get some sleep

Insufficient sleep is becoming a public health problem in the UK. The recommended amount of sleep is 7.7 hours a night, and studies suggest that Britons are under-sleeping by around one hour each night at 6.8 hours.[8] Teachers on the other hand are even worse: studies suggest that teachers are getting a meagre 6 hours sleep a night, and that the quality of sleep is often poor.[9] Much of this is due to the inability of teachers to switch off. Be it the poorly behaved class we may teach or the constant need to explain and defend ourselves to somebody, there is always something on our minds.

Lack of sleep takes a huge toll on the body and mind. On the physical side, in the long run, it can increase chances of impaired immunity, early aging, weight gain, hypertension and diabetes. You may read these and not feel any immediate threat, as you may only be young and consider them to be merely a distant possibility. You cannot however, and no teacher should, ignore the more immediate effects of sleep deprivation, which include irritability, forgetfulness, less efficient organisation and planning, and higher cortisol (which will make you feel more stressed and has a whole range of other negative effects of itself).[10] In short, sleep deprivation is counterproductive to teaching and potentially life-threatening. There is nothing hardcore about 'just getting on with it'. Hit the sack.

One of the causes of the lack of sleep, not just for teachers, is the use of smartphones in bed before sleeping. Melatonin is a hormone involved in sleep and humans have a natural circadian rhythm that causes our bodies to produce melatonin during darkness, thereby encouraging sleep at night rather than during the day. The blue light emitted by smartphones decreases melatonin production.[11] So in effect, by looking at a smartphone before bed, you are telling your brain to remain alert and active.

Put the phone away at least an hour before bed. Make sure you get some downtime before sleeping, perhaps by reading a book (the ones with pages which you have to physically turn) and try to avoid devices where you are looking directly into a light source. If it is essential for you to do work, exercise, or any other intense activity late in the evening, make sure you get an hour of relaxation prior to sleeping.

As in the previous sections, it is essential to mention here that you may just not be able to get the amount of sleep you want, perhaps due to having young children or other dependents. If it is absolutely impossible for you to get the required amount of sleep, invest in some cherry extracts. These are inexpensive and contain melatonin. Cherry extracts are known to help improve the quality of the sleep that you do get.[12] It is also worth noting that sleep is cumulative: if you lose sleep on Thursday, try and make it back on a Friday as this should lessen the damage and improve your overall wellbeing.[13]

Exercise, exercise, exercise!

One of the main (and justified) complaints from teachers is tiredness. When you begin teaching, you soon learn that going out on a Friday night is out of the question and during the last week of the winter term, you are literally forcing yourself to work. You cannot physically take any more. Or can you?

Teaching is a job that is high in what psychologists refer to as 'emotional labour'. This can be described as the process of managing feelings and expressions to fulfil the emotional requirements of a job.[14] In plain English, this refers to the way you feel when you've just had a challenging group who danced circles around you, and you practically stapled your lips together to stop yourself losing your job by saying something you'd regret. You taught your nice group immediately afterwards and you forced yourself into a happy mood because you knew it wouldn't be right to take your anger out on them. This is emotional labour: the constant managing of emotions during work. While other factors also play a role, much of why you are so tired is because of this.

The benefits of exercise are countless, but there are two main reasons why a teacher should embrace exercise: it reduces stress thereby making you happy, and it gives you more energy. During exercise, endorphins are released which promote positive thinking, confidence, and an overall sense of wellbeing.[15] These effects continue even on the days you are not working out. Teachers often get into a negative spiral and we all know that with constant scrutiny, pressure to reach targets, and an ever-increasing workload, this is easily done. Exercise will enable you to take control of your mental state and not become a victim of it. Many people are surprised by the fact that exercise gives you more energy overall, as they often view exercise as something that requires (and therefore exhausts) energy. The reality is that both are true: the more active you are, the more active you can be.[16] A regular workout routine will help keep you energetic in the classroom as well as when working on your buns of steel.

Guidelines for exercise vary, but 150 minutes each week over 3-4 sessions is perfectly adequate.[17] As said earlier, you don't have to join a gym: you could just go running for 20 minutes, or do a high-intensity interval training (HIIT) workout for 30 minutes with nothing but an exercise mat. Working out with others is proven to be even more beneficial for many reasons, including morale, camaraderie and competition, and this is probably why it is common in schools to have Friday football or netball. If your school is lacking in this, why not take the initiative to start something up? The reason most teachers (and perhaps most people) give for not exercising is a lack of time but hopefully after reading this chapter you will become more efficient with your time-management. Try also not to have all-or-nothing thinking: if it is absolutely impossible for you to get a good amount of exercise, remember that some is better than none. So get some!

Eat healthy

Your mind and body take a beating from teaching so it is important that you don't beat yourself up further by having a poor diet. Begin the day with a high carb breakfast to provide you with the slow release energy to get you through to break/lunchtime. Eat a good amount of green leafy vegetables to provide you with iron, an essential mineral in preventing fatigue.[18] Keep the sugar and caffeine to a minimum. These may taste nice and give you a sudden burst of energy, but it wears off pretty quickly and you feel even more tired and sluggish after. They are also known to increase anxiety.[19] Many vegetables and fruits on the other hand have the exact opposite effect, so make sure you get your seven (yes, seven – they changed it) servings of fruit and vegetables a day, with more veg than fruit as they are lower in sugar. The vitamins and minerals present in these are essential for the repair process that your body is screaming for.[20] There is much research to suggest that working more than 40 hours a week negatively impacts one's health,[21] so it is therefore reasonable to conclude that a teacher working around 55 hours a week should be extra careful. Don't add to the damage. You will look, feel, and actually *be* healthier if you follow all the health guidelines that you didn't when you were at uni. By all means get yourself a big fat kebab on the weekend, but keep it plant-based Monday to Friday.

Prioritising and Workload Management

Unless you work for around 70 hours a week, it is inevitable that there is something you will be behind on, haven't done or have plain forgotten to do. Since your training years you have been told to prioritise, but you constantly feel that you are prioritising everything and therefore by its very definition, you are not actually prioritising at all! Hopefully this section will help you to prioritise correctly.

Prioritise the visible

If you have a report deadline looming, a book scrutiny waiting or a learning walk impending, then these should be your priority as they are the ones you will be judged by. You may think (and rightly so, in my opinion) that this is unfair: all books should be marked at the same rate and all lessons should be the same, irrespective of who is watching. I couldn't agree with you more, however, reality dictates otherwise. The fact is that your entire practice is going to be judged by what is visible to your line managers, and by prioritising what they see, you avoid harming your professional reputation by being judged harshly. This may be obvious to some, but there are many teachers who get themselves into an avoidable pickle by spending hours marking year 7 books when they're being observed with their year 11 the next day. Just play the game. You can catch up with anything after your observation. It doesn't make you a bad teacher, just a smart one. Work smart.

Planning is better than marking

If something has got to give, it is better for it to be marking than planning. Ofsted have recently changed their opinion on the impact of marking, claiming it is far less than once thought. Pupils on the other hand have always been consistent in their view. Yes, they do want feedback, grades and so on, but what they want more is consistently engaging and relevant lessons, and a teacher with whom they have a good relationship. If your planning slips, the consequences can be worse than if your marking does. The class may misbehave, they may tell everyone you're a crap teacher, they may even lose respect for you, especially if you're consistently ill-prepared. Delayed marking, however, is easily forgiven if you're otherwise a good teacher. Obviously this advice does not apply if you're about to have a book scrutiny, but in general if you are pressed for time and have to do one or the other, planning is better than marking.

Do the easy stuff when you're tired

Assume you have a class set of exam papers to mark. The first four pages are multiple choice (so all you have to do is put a tick or a cross next to them) and the rest of the questions involve longer answers. It would be a good idea to mark just the first four pages separately from the rest. You may want to do these at the end of the day when you're less inclined to mentally engage, and save the more difficult marking for the morning. You may prefer the exact opposite. Whatever your preference, the key here is self-awareness. Don't create unnecessary hurdles and don't slog it out if there's an easier way.

Don't waste your free periods

Have a plan for exactly what you are going to do in your free periods and stick to it. Avoid the temptation to socialise too much during free periods and make sure you have enough to do to take up the whole time. Remember, if you don't do it in your frees, it ultimately means more work at home. You will no doubt get distracted by colleagues, particularly if you have to work in a common area, and it can be difficult to get on with your work while at the same time trying not to appear antisocial. If colleagues try to continuously talk to you while you are trying to work, a simple 'Hang on a sec, let me just finish this' (with no eye contact) should give them a polite hint. The lack of eye contact emphasises that you are engrossed in a task and it also conveys the message in a somewhat gentler way. If you want more free time at home, save the socialising for lunchtime.

To-do lists

Some teachers' organisation requires organisation: they have a notebook, a planner, a calendar, a folder, a ring binder and four different folders on their email account. One suggestion is to be organised but keep it simple. Make a to-do list in one location only. A to-do list may last the entire week, so be sure to keep referring to it and adding or crossing stuff off constantly. Add to your to-do list the moment you know about the task, don't wait, or you'll end up forgetting. If you cross stuff off of your to-do list the moment you've completed the task, you will gain a sense of completion and therefore satisfaction.

To-do lists are like the Hydra: you cut off one head and two more grow in its place. But this is the unavoidable nature of the teaching beast. Pace yourself and do things one at a time and always have a backup plan. For example, if you come into work early to do something which involves the internet and the system at your school is unreliable, make sure you have some marking or something to fall back on lest you find yourself very frustrated.

Emails

Most emails you receive can be deleted at a glance, so get into the habit of deleting them there and then. Even if you are teaching, spending literally 2 minutes deleting emails every lesson alleviates that sense of panic you get when you check them at the end of the day and you have 40 unread emails in your inbox (35 of which are irrelevant to you). If you notice an important lengthy email that requires your attention, put it on your to-do list, then check it when you have time. The ability to multitask varies from person to person, however, when most people do decide to multitask, no one task is done effectively. Save the long emails for when you don't have 30 kids in front of you.

Breaks and lunches

Breaks and lunches are your time. Yours. Nobody else's. Recuperation is done during rest, and bypassing it continuously can lead to a series of physical and mental problems, too many to discuss here. Avoid working during break and lunch and try not to be alone during these times. Instead, use these times to have a laugh with your colleagues. Did you know that Ofsted are prohibited from entering the staffroom? Why do you think this is? Because it's simply none of their business! As long as you are not doing anything that upsets your colleagues or seriously harms your professionalism, go all out during break times. Many teachers stay for years at the most difficult schools because of the relationships they have built and the banter they have with their colleagues. Develop these relationships, and laugh. Laugh loudly. Be immature. A short time ago I, aged 36, and a 52-year-old colleague spent an entire lunchtime arm-wrestling. We all were laughing to the point of tears. How do you think we felt while teaching after that? Laughter is medically proven to decrease stress hormones and increase immune cells and endorphins.[22] Even if you are a reserved individual, consciously look for opportunities to laugh.

Having said the above, the expectation to do some form of work (intervention, detentions, mentoring and so on) during breaks or lunches is becoming increasingly common. If it is not the norm at your school then you needn't bother, however if it is, keep it to once a week. Anything more than that may make you look good in the short-term, but it wont be long before you are either exhausted, resentful or both. Save lunchtime for food and laughter.

Holidays

You should consider the holidays sacrosanct as they are the payback for the 55 hour term-time working week. A recent study showed that teachers must relax over the holidays to avoid exhaustion and to 'restore their emotional energy'. As a teacher, this obviously comes as no surprise to you, but now you have the proof when your non-teacher friends tell you how easy (they think) you've got it! As said previously, teachers struggle to switch off from work even during the holidays. To avoid this, try to actively relax: do something you enjoy. Even if it's eating large quantities of bad food and watching trash TV, you're still relaxed and engaging in something. If you just wake up and see where the day takes you, you risk your mind wandering and ultimately thinking about work, or you may come to the end of the holiday and realise you've wasted all the time which you were so eager to have just a few weeks ago.

Any work you do in the holidays must be accidental. This means you should try your utmost to get everything done during term time and only the bits that you absolutely cannot do should be reserved for the holidays. If it is essential for you to work, then restrict it to one day in a half term, and two days in a long holiday. Do all the work in those times and do it at school where possible. Long bouts of work in restricted time periods make it easier to switch off for the rest of the holiday. If however you prefer a more staggered approach, then make sure you compartmentalise appropriately. Get the work out of the way early in the morning for example, then spend the rest of the day actively relaxing. Don't just allow the work to happen to you.

9.

Bullying: the Problem and the Solution

As in any other workplace, bullying in teaching is a reality. While it may not be common enough to warrant paranoia, it is common enough for it to be discussed. Generic workplace bullying advice would not really meet the needs of a teacher, so omitting specifics from the (Un)official Teacher's Manual would be doing a great disservice. This chapter aims to define bullying, describe the methods used by bullies, and hopefully give some useful tips on how to avoid being bullied. Finally, some advice will be given as to what to do if you ever find yourself in such a dire situation. Before you begin, I'd like to remind you to maintain a holistic approach to the book: this chapter is not nice. If you are not quite in the profession or relatively new, you do run the risk of being put off. In light of this, I ask here that you not forget about the numerous rewards a career in teaching can offer. The aim of this chapter is not for you to walk around school in fear, terrified of the intentions of anyone and everyone. It is to make you aware so that you can avoid, pre-empt, and generally be one step ahead of the game and remain a happy and productive teacher.

What is bullying?

According to the Health and Safety Executive (HSE) website, there is no legal definition of workplace bullying, but it is a commonly held view that bullying involves negative behaviour being targeted at an individual or individuals, repeatedly and persistently over time.[23] While 'negative behaviour' is a term vague in nature, this chapter will tell you exactly what type of behaviour to look out for in schools. At this stage, it is important to emphasise the concept of 'repeatedly and persistently': if someone punches you and takes your money one day, then you got mugged. If that same person does it every week, then you are being bullied. The same thing applies in schools. If you find yourself being a victim of anything described in this chapter, it generally only constitutes bullying if it is repeated and persistent. Have that in mind throughout, lest you jump to conclusions.

Who bullies?

Bullying usually involves an abuse of power, so it may be instigated by those in positions above you, in other words middle or senior leaders. There are cases where people bully people in the same hierarchy position, and this can impact on your day-to-day life. This type of bullying may not however be a hindrance to your career as long as the person(s) are acting alone and not with someone above you in position.

Why do they bully?

The primary reason for bullying in schools is due to pressure. The pressure to achieve government targets is at the heart of the repeated and persistent negative behaviour characterised in bullying. This might not be obvious in any particular bullying scenario, but you can be sure that it exists underneath the surface. This does however, come with a health warning: bullying is never justified and we cannot and should not treat the perpetrator as the victim irrespective of the 'reasons'.

Who Gets Bullied and How to Avoid it

Bullying on the grounds of race, religion, gender, sexuality or disability are not among the common reasons for bullying in the teaching profession. Although such incidences do occur and should not be ignored, in teaching you are far more likely to get bullied for repeatedly challenging your Headteacher than you are for being black, Muslim, female, gay or disabled. Some of the most common reasons for bullying are:

Challenging the leadership team

Some leaders, middle or senior, simply do not like being challenged. Teachers may perceive their ideas as poor, or their demands as ridiculous, and speak up against them. They can do this privately via talking to colleagues, or they can do this publicly by arguing at meetings. They may even outright refrain from doing non-compulsory tasks. Teachers who regularly challenge the leadership team can be seen as problematic, particularly if they are supported by other staff. Often, teachers will *want* to challenge the leadership team but won't, and what follows is this: the teacher who does speak up inspires others to do the same, thus multiplying the school leaders' problems. The leaders then will then, to put it crudely, cut the head off of the snake.

They say you're not good enough

This means many things to many people, particularly school leaders. Allow me to explain: some schools have unreasonably 'high' (inverted commas are used here because if something is not sustainable, it is definitely not

94

commendable and therefore not actually high) expectations of their staff. They will demand, by hook or by crook, morning, break, lunch, after school, weekend and holiday intervention sessions, as well as bombarding their staff with an unreasonable amount of scrutiny. They may also perpetuate a belief among their staff that good teaching can only be practiced one way – their way. They will continue with this despite their staff turnover being high, as many staff will leave of their own accord. On the surface they will insist that xyz is optional, but the not-so-nice surprise for those that don't do as they're told is to be bullied out.

Perceived bullying when you really aren't good enough

There is a very fine line between the previous section and this section, which is why in some cases of bullying, the victim is not necessarily an entirely innocent victim. For example, there was a teacher who used to agitate her colleagues by speaking to them abruptly. She only marked her books when she absolutely had to and pupils would often complain that in her lessons she would simply hand out a textbook and sit at her laptop. Prior to the arrival of the new Head of Department, her antics had gone unchecked for a couple of years. During a book scrutiny she claimed to have left her books in her car. The Head of Department decided that enough was enough and the Headteacher was informed. The Headteacher walked with her to her car to get the books and, not surprisingly, they were unmarked. The teacher was instantaneously put on capability proceedings. She immediately claimed she was being bullied, but her colleagues on the other hand knew she had it coming for a long time, and were actually quite relieved that she could no longer get away with murder.

While bullying is never justified, it *is* fully justified to take action against a teacher who is doing a disservice to children and fellow colleagues. The previous scenario is not an example of bullying no matter how much the victim insists that it is. It would be considered bullying, however, had the capability proceedings not been followed correctly and if the teacher wasn't given a chance to improve.

Jealousy, envy, and vindictiveness

You may have never challenged the leadership team in your life. Your observations may always be good or better and your marking may be exemplary. Yet you can still find yourself being bullied. If this is the case, then you are likely to be the victim of a genuine to the core bully. This person has just got it in for you and possibly others, and they are usually motivated by some combination of jealousy, envy, and vindictiveness. Here are a couple of examples:

- A new teacher showed good practice during learning walks and observations. The Head sang his praises during meetings, and this was a Headteacher who was known to be very reserved with praise. The bullying soon began, perpetrated by middle leaders.

- Many of the younger female teachers in a particular department felt that their Head of Department was deliberately targeting them for extra work. These teachers were married with children but the Head of Department, who was a woman much older than them, had neither children nor a significant other. Just like the previous example, these teachers felt that they were unfairly targeted due to the jealousy of the perpetrator.

You can become unlucky and have to endure working with an individual who just has an axe to grind with you for no tangible reason. On the positive side, a bully like this usually has many targets so they are much easier to deal with, as you will have a lot of backup.

Bullying Tactics

So what tactics are employed by adult school bullies to let their victim know that their presence at the school is no longer wanted? Be bully-savvy by familiarising yourself with the following bullying tactics:

Timetabling

In secondary schools, the most favoured method used by leadership teams to bully their staff is timetabling. Timetabling and rooming are details which most teachers do not understand the intricacies of, and for this reason they are an easy tool for bullying. Because you don't know it, when you question it, you have no way of verifying the lies they tell you regarding it. This can be illustrated by an example:

At a particular school, it was common for teachers to do Saturday revision sessions (albeit paid) for their GCSE groups. This was encouraged by the leadership team, whose answer to any workload complaint was 'We do what's best for the kids' – a seemingly noble statement, manufactured to enable any unjust action to be taken against any teacher.

So in doing 'what's best for the kids', any staff that were not doing Saturday sessions were bullied out. Of course the Headteacher, who was described by his staff as a 'charming sociopath', was always insisting that Saturday sessions were voluntary and that he was respectful of his staff's personal time (blah, blah, blah). At the same time however, the constant bombardment with statements such as 'These kids have GOT to get Cs!' from the Deputy Head (Heads and Deputy Heads often play good-cop, bad-cop) meant that staff pretty much had no choice. Teachers who did not do the sessions were deprived of year 11 classes the following year, and in some cases deprived of even their own classroom: one bullied teacher was teaching entirely KS3 groups and had 20 different classrooms to teach in. Not a single lesson was in the same location. Obviously the stress of this, combined with the obvious disdain from the management team caused him much distress and eventually led to him leaving the profession.

Excessive scrutiny

As mentioned in an earlier chapter, if you try your hardest to catch a teacher out, you will. Due to the volume of work and the fact that a day only consists of 24 hours, it is inevitable that something or other will not be done to the best of your ability. Repeated scrutiny is one way of trying to catch out and therefore bully teachers by making them look incompetent, when in reality they are as 'incompetent' as anybody else.

For example, there was a teacher who regularly complained about tasks that he deemed unnecessary and bureaucratic in nature. He was popular with staff and they often supported him in his disputes with middle and senior leaders. While the leadership team paid lip service to his concerns in public, behind the scenes, they decided to go after him. When they conducted learning walks, they dropped in on him more times than everyone else. When he was observed for his performance management, they stayed in his lesson for 15 minutes longer than the required time, claiming something vague such as 'We wanted to see the conclusion to the lesson'. In addition to this, the Headteacher would randomly come into his lessons, check a couple of books, frown, and then walk away without saying anything. While there was nothing they could officially do, as they didn't actually happen to catch him out, the fact that they desperately tried to is enough to constitute bullying. When faced with excessive scrutiny, be aware that this is a common complaint from many teachers at many schools; it only constitutes bullying if it is directed only at individuals without any tangible reason.

Malicious scrutiny

Rather than excessively scrutinise, some schools choose to maliciously scrutinise in order to bully staff. One teacher reported that a Deputy Head decided she had it in for him. She would speak to underachieving pupils in his class and ask leading questions such as 'Is your lack of progress due to Sir's poor teaching?'

Another experienced teacher and middle leader said she felt it no coincidence that the moment she challenged the leadership team's decisions, her observations came out as 'requiring improvement'. As an experienced teacher she knew full well they were 'good'.

A third teacher reported that random book checks were taking place and staff were asked to leave their marked books visible so that the Head of Department could take a random sample. He was later informed by a close colleague that the Head of Department went through his stack of books with the aim of finding an unmarked book, rather than just grabbing a random sample as he did for the other teachers in the department.

Over-punishment

Assume you did miss out on some marking and it was noticed during a scrutiny. If you find yourself on a six week 'informal' action plan, or sitting in the Deputy Head's office with three different members of the leadership team staring at you, then it is likely that you are being bullied.

Withholding pay progression

Achieving pay progression at most schools requires a combination of data and evidence. Those in the profession know that the vast majority of the time, pay progression is not automatic but involves a judgement call. A member of staff who is declined pay progression but achieved the same results and provided the same evidence as someone who was awarded it, may well be the victim of bullying.

Awkwardness

While this is difficult to define, you know it when you experience it. If persistent, it is likely to be deliberate in nature and its purpose is to make your life just that little bit (or a lot) more difficult. Bullied teachers often speak about:

Mysterious emails

The Head emails you on a Friday night telling you to come and see them on Monday. There is no other information in the email.

Cancelled meetings

A bullied teacher was asked to 'pop down to the Head's office for a quick chat' at 5pm. The Head knew full well that the teacher normally left at 4pm due to personal commitments. When the teacher turned up at 5pm, the Head was not there.

Obscured scrutiny

A teacher was scheduled to be observed period 3. The observer showed up period 2 and claimed she got it wrong but nonetheless continued to observe. She stayed for period 2 and 3.

Withholding information

A Head of Department was repeatedly not told about changes being made to her department until her knowledge of them became absolutely necessary. Even her team knew before her, because the Assistant Head (her line manager) was pally with her team and would tell them everything while disregarding the needs of the Head of Department. Her team hence lost confidence in her. Thus, it was made easier to get rid of her when they 'restructured' later on.

This one takes the cake

A Head of Department refused to share a worksheet with a teacher on the grounds that it was her 'intellectual property'[24] – I'm not too sure how to categorise this one!

Aggression

They will hopefully never punch you and steal your lunch money, but some adult school bullies are outright aggressive. People's perception of aggression can vary and it is important that you are aware that the following behaviours are unacceptable:

Shouting/swearing

A teacher once reported that a Head of Department told her to 'read the fucking mark scheme'.[25]

Undermining

A teacher was humiliated by his Head of Department in the presence of colleagues for his marking not being 'up to scratch'. Another teacher, also in the presence of colleagues, was abruptly told to do up his top button. Such actions should be taken in private, never in public.

Harassment via email

A teacher who was struggling with the classroom management of a particularly poorly behaved group was constantly receiving emails from her seniors questioning her actions. There were multiple emails throughout the day and they had many others cc'd into them. Another teacher reported being repeatedly undermined and humiliated by the Head of Department who would quash her ideas with the 'reply all' response.[25]

Body language

A teacher was being pressured to do 'optional' Saturday revision sessions. The Assistant Head would approach him and ask him which Saturday to put him down for. When he refused, the Assistant Head would stare at him for 15 seconds straight. Another teacher would leave the school premises at 3:30pm. The Headteacher would see him leave, look at his watch, then look at him with an expression of confusion.

What to Do About Bullying

There is no step-by-step formula for dealing with bullying, as every situation is unique and consists of many variables beyond the capacity of this chapter. What follows is generic advice on how to avoid being bullied (as prevention is better than cure) and what to do if you do end up in this unfortunate situation.

Make sure you are a good practitioner

This is your weapon of mass destruction. If you have followed the advice throughout this book, you will hopefully avoid the risk of having negative attention being drawn towards you. Most school leaders, even the bullies, claim always to be acting in the interests of the children. If you are too, then the likelihood of you being viewed as a problem will decrease significantly. Surely nobody would be foolish enough to get rid of a good teacher?

Effectively challenge the leadership team

You are teaching day in, day out. For you to not be able to challenge a decision, made by someone else, that will directly affect you is outright offensive, and that is being said with no hyperbole whatsoever. If you deem an idea or practice to be ridiculous, untenable or so on, then you should bloody well say so because you know your craft well and your knowledge demands respect. If you are careful, you *can* challenge the leadership team without the risk of being bullied.

How? Firstly, you must be a strong, established teacher. Whoever you are challenging must be aware of this and the better your professional reputation, the more seriously you will be taken and the less likely you are to be bullied. If you are even slightly unsure of how you are perceived, play it safe and keep your mouth shut. Secondly, do not act alone. If you have decided that doing break time intervention is unreasonable and all of your colleagues are still doing it, then you will be viewed as problematic and you risk blowback if you don't. There is no glory in martyrdom. Instead, make sure others are of the same opinion as you and, more importantly, are willing to back your case through words and action. Thirdly, leave emotion at the door. Your ranting is fully justified to you and perhaps your colleagues, but often in the eyes of leadership teams, ranting is synonymous with negativity. If you want to complain, apply logic and reason and appear to have sense of purpose. Saying 'There's absolutely no point in doing that!' sounds far worse than 'I'm struggling to see how this benefits pupil progress'. It is also important to know the written and unwritten expectations of your school. Stick to these guidelines and those in Chapter 4 and you should be ok. So challenge the leadership team! Just don't make a hobby of it!

Get it in writing

If bullying starts, it is useful to have everything in writing, particularly if you decide to take action. Where possible, try and get the bully to put their pesky requests in writing. A simple 'Sorry, I've got such a terrible memory – do you mind dropping me an email?' should do the trick. Be sure, if you do decide to fight, the bully will cleverly deny everything. Have as much physical evidence as you can.

Contact your union representative

This should be a no-brainer. Your union rep will know the people and systems much better than you and so will be able to give you situation-specific advice.

Report it

Whether or not you decide to report a bully is a judgement call that only you can make, however it is important that you manage your expectations. Teachers who complain to the Head about bullying (unless the bully is the Head, of course) often report that the Head will listen, appearing greatly concerned, but will ultimately pacify the member of staff by trivialising their concerns. The Head may say things like 'He can be rude sometimes but he doesn't always mean it. He's just very passionate about his job and gets carried away'.

Often Headteachers have a need to show staff that the leadership team is united, and in doing so they do not overtly take the teacher's side. Instead they provide slight support, or an illusion of it, depending on how cynical you want to be! Either that, or bullying is part of their 'management' strategy and they are outright complicit in it.

Allow me to reiterate: the message here is not to refrain from reporting, but rather to manage your expectations. If however the bullying has no basis, or perceived basis, in your professionalism, then you should get the full support of your Head 100% of the time. By and large, Headteachers do not want their staff to be miserable and they do act properly against the jealous, envious or vindictive bullies described earlier.

Stick up for yourself

This particularly applies when you are dealing with a bully who verbally assaults you. Clench your jaw, get *Eye of the Tiger* playing in your head if you have to, before saying 'I'm NOT going to be spoken to like that'. Then walk away and await a possible apology. There is absolutely nothing wrong with demanding dignity and respect in the workplace and your school probably has a policy in place to protect you.

Stress leave

If you absolutely cannot take it any more, then see your doctor and act on their advice. Be mindful however, that if you do decide to take time off, it will go on your employment record and may affect future employment prospects. Balance this potential consequence with protecting your mental and physical health. Again, this is a judgement call and only you can make it, but don't take unnecessary risks with either your mental health, or your future employment.

Leave

The bullying might only be temporary, but even once it's over, bullied staff often report having built up so much resentment that they find themselves fearful, cynical and just unable to function in the same school. In cases of historical or ongoing bullying, it is perfectly ok and often even advisable just to leave. The difficult bit, however, is to eat humble pie and do exactly as you are told until then. It is likely that your bullies are the ones who will be writing your reference, so the last thing you want is for them to show you just how vindictive they can be. Knuckle down, stay on track, and start applying. Just because you have not thrived at your current school it doesn't mean you won't elsewhere. Many staff who leave a dire situation can and do go on to bigger and better things.

10.

How to Get the Teaching Job You Want

Whether you've decided to leave your current school, or have just finished your training and are looking for your first post, getting the job you want can be seamless if the correct steps are followed:

Visit the school

Assume you have seen an advert at a school you like the sound of and are considering applying. It is important that you visit the school prior to submitting your application and there are two main reasons for this.

Firstly, you get a chance to make a good impression before the interview as your enthusiasm will be self-evident; the fact that you went all the way there means you are someone who makes decisions wholeheartedly. Also, from looking at the advert, you will know that they have general requirements as well as specific ones, and by visiting beforehand you will be able to drop subtle hints as to how you meet their specific requirements. For example, if the ad says 'ability to teach KS5 BTEC is desirable' you can mention to the person showing you around that you have a lot of experience in this, or it's something you've been eager to do for a long time. You greatly increase the likelihood of being offered an interview if you visit the school prior to application.

Secondly, you get a chance to form an opinion on the school: it's a two way process. You are going to be spending the majority of your waking life working there, so it's important you have enough information to decide whether or not the school is for you. The advert is never going to tell you that the Head of Department is off with stress, they are understaffed, and you will be sharing a corridor with four supply teachers. Make the most of the visit. Stick your head in some classrooms, observe pupil movement during breaks or lunchtime. Talk to staff, but try not to be too intrusive or controversial as everything you ask will be reported (or just gossiped) back to somebody, so it's better to keep it general. When you've finished the visit, go by your gut feeling. If it's a yes, give them the application there and then. If it's a no, thank them for the visit and say you'll be in touch.

Get inside information

School visits are usually brief and you just cannot get all of the information you want. Networking is key and it is no secret that teachers are the greatest of gossips. The more people you talk to, the more likely you are to come across someone who knows someone who works at the school. Teachers by and large are supportive of each other, so that person would most likely be happy to speak to you. Ask them the exact planning requirements, behaviour policy and so on, so you can produce an outstanding lesson on your interview day. The more you know about the school the more impressed the interviewers will be. Start networking as soon as you consider applying.

The Interview

There are a multitude of articles that tell you the type of questions that are asked at teaching interviews, as well as the answers expected for them. The aim of this section is not to rehash those, but to give you some not-so-obvious interview tips.

Don't ramble, just answer the question

Teachers love to talk, but not everyone wants to listen. On a given interview day as many as 10 potential employees can be interviewed. It is therefore important that your answers are succinct, memorable and backed up with evidence. For example, if you are asked to 'Describe a lesson where you made your subject engaging to SEN pupils' answer it like this:

'There are two examples that come to mind. Firstly, last year when I taught a low ability group, I took them to my car to show them how to check the oil, showing them the implication of temperature on pressure. The kids really enjoyed it because it was practical and relevant to their daily life. Secondly...'

All too many teachers end up continuously rambling, without pausing, without making eye contact, and using more words than necessary. If you want to be remembered, be succinct. When your answer dictates, make eye contact, smile, pause, and get to the point! Also, many teachers misunderstand the question and end up giving an entirely irrelevant answer. It is perfectly fine to ask for a question to be repeated or to request a moment to think before you answer. You don't have to blurt it all out and hope that it's right.

It is worth noting that if an interview doesn't quite go your way, at the end of the interview say 'Please may I say something in support of my application?'

Then tell them anything you feel you missed. They are unlikely to say no, and it may just tip their decision in your favour. It's worth a shot.

Visible evidence

This is more for experienced teachers, or exceptional trainees. Bring a brief portfolio with you, containing anything that will make you appear an excellent practitioner. You could include:

- A copy of the feedback form from a good or outstanding lesson, highlighted as appropriate
- Photos of you working with pupils during something extracurricular
- Any correspondence you may have had from a Headteacher praising your practice
- Feedback forms or certificates from INSETs you may have run or attended

If it doesn't involve too much faffing around, refer to these briefly as you speak about them. Visible evidence will help you stand out.

Be quirky (if it's in your nature)

Some teachers who are quirky or eccentric by nature tend to shy away from their own personality during job interviews. For example, let's suppose you are a science teacher and would happily wear a periodic table or Einstein tie: don't shy away from that in your interview! Schools look for teachers with a sense of humour and a passion for their subject. The quirky tie ticks both boxes. Be careful though: if you have to phone up seven of your friends to ask them if you should do or wear xyz on your interview, then you probably shouldn't. There can be a fine line. Be true to yourself but at the same time don't come across as a potential liability.

The student panel

With 'pupil voice' being high on the government agenda, schools will often ask a group of pupils to interview potential staff. These will usually be the school elites, and they will have similar judgement criteria to any adult interviewing you. Hence, you don't have to worry about not being seen as a 'safe' teacher in their eyes. What students will perhaps be hotter on than even school leaders is your stage presence, your ability to build relationships and (depending upon the school) your ability to manage behaviour. Make sure these are in check by displaying a combination of confidence, a sense of humour, and a genuine interest in the pupils in your care. The need to be clear and succinct in your answers is of paramount importance, as even the most intellectual kids have low concentration spans. Adults struggle to listen to a waffler, but kids will just switch off. When the interview is over, they will be asked questions like 'Would you want to be taught by her?' or 'Do you think he could deal with poor behaviour?', so it's important to make a lasting positive impression.

In the staffroom

It is common on interview days for interviewees to be subtly left in a common area with other staff while they are eating lunch, working, or just hanging out. While this will never be put on the itinerary, it is deliberate and actually part of the interview process. They are observing how you relate to people and thus what you would be like to work with. If you are ever in this situation, don't fall for the trap of assuming you have to sit there like a timid mouse. Talk to people! Listen, ask questions, converse, show your sense of humour. It's all good. The only time it isn't is if you are obnoxious, arrogant, offensive, rude, or overly opinionated. When you have left, they will all be asked 'What's he/she like?' or 'Would he/she be easy to work with?' – at least wait until you've got the job before you show your true colours.

11.

Maintaining Good Relationships

The importance of working relationships in a school cannot be overstated. How well you relate to support staff, fellow teachers, middle leaders and senior leaders will almost always be directly proportional to how happy you are at school. It may be the factor that can lead to your promotion or even your professional demise. Like any other relationship, there are usually some unwritten boundaries that both parties cannot and should not cross. Conversely, there are also some unwritten behaviours that would help to cultivate a positive relationship. This chapter is aimed at a standard classroom teacher and sets out guidance for maintaining good relationships.

With Fellow Teachers

Being happy at work involves eliminating, or at least not creating, unnecessary conflict, drama and so on. Your colleagues may be people who you wouldn't befriend under normal circumstances, but you do have to see them every day, so the more you get on with them the easier all your lives will be.

Don't undermine them

What this essentially means is don't do anything that will negatively impact your colleagues' professionalism. Here is an example of one type of undermining behaviour to avoid, followed by some suggestions for alternative actions:

- Mr Jones was sharing a year 8 maths class with Ms Smith. The class mentioned in passing to Ms Smith that they didn't understand the algebra topic that Mr Jones was teaching them. During break time that day, Ms Smith said to Mr Jones, in the midst of a crowded staffroom, 'The kids don't understand algebra. You may want to teach it again'

Ms Smith may have had the best interest of the children at heart, but what Mr Jones hears is that he's incompetent, and to add insult to injury, the whole department now knows it too. It would have been better if Ms Smith told the kids to take it up with Mr Jones themselves. Failing that, she should have told him in private, in the politest way possible. This is just one example of the many ways in which you can unwittingly (or if you are malicious, deliberately) undermine a fellow colleague. Think before you speak. If in doubt, shut up! Unless you are a middle leader, it's not your job to pass judgement on your colleagues. Obviously, if you have serious concerns, then report them, but never take it on yourself.

Big them up

Kids will speak about good teachers. If you hear something good about one of your colleagues, tell them and make sure others can hear you: the exact opposite of the previous scenario. The colleague will associate the positive feelings evoked with you, will take a better liking to you, and will therefore be more likely to support you if ever you need it. A characteristic trait of insecure people is that they never say positive things about others as they feel it somehow diminishes their own work. You don't want to be like them do you? Big up your colleagues, but don't overdo it as it may come across as fake.

Support them

Don't be stingy with your resources. If you can see somebody is planning a lesson that you have already planned, offer to share it. If you can see they are stressed after a difficult class, lend a supportive ear. If their car has broken down in the car park, offer them a lift home. If they have lost their keys, send an email to the department. Supportive behaviour breeds supportive behaviour: be as supportive as your circumstances allow you to be. You won't be able to be Mother Teresa, but Oprah Winfrey is a reasonable aim.

Be humble

With educational jargon, pedagogy and professional expectations constantly changing, it is inevitable that some people will be more clued up than others at any particular time. Remember two things: First, just because you are aware of xyz, it doesn't mean you are better than someone who isn't. Second, your way is your way – not *the* way. There is more than one way to skin a cat, so to speak. Don't be overly incessant on your correctness with regard to teaching and learning. People don't want to work with arrogant people, and no matter how many good ideas one may have, if the messenger is not liked, the ideas will most probably be shot down. Be humble.

With Your Head of Department

With regards to your daily teaching and possible progression, your Head of Department is your first port of call. Have no doubt, what they think of you matters. So how do you ensure a good working relationship?

Don't keep bugging them

Saying that Heads of Department are busy people is neither an overstatement nor a revelation. The more independently their staff can work, the happier they are and by default, the happier they are with you. Your Head of Department is there to support you and you must ask for support as and when necessary. However, it is not in your interest to use them as a first port of call for trivialities. For example, let's say you accidently deleted an important email from them. Ask someone else to forward it to you, not them! Let's say you don't have the mark scheme to a particular test, but you know others do: ask them, not your Head of Department. Obviously you will have to use your own discretion and act in accordance with the culture of your school, but in general if someone else can help you with it, ask them first.

Don't go above their head

Unless your Head of Department is poorly organised to the point that it is causing you unbearable anxiety, do not go above their head. This means you must not complain to a senior leader about a middle leader unless under the circumstance described. The toughest place to be in a school is in the middle, so it is inevitable that not every Head of Department is going to have everything done perfectly. You have to be somewhat forgiving, as going above their head may have serious repercussions. Keep it in-house. If you are friendly with anyone on the leadership team, take care to avoid making throwaway comments that may make your Head of Department look bad. If ever you are prodded for information, just tell them everything is fine or better.

Relax, but be professional

Your Head of Department will see you every day, so it will be difficult for you to not be yourself. Not that there is anything wrong with being yourself, but there are some behaviours you should avoid with regards to your professionalism. You would probably be ok with, for example, telling a fellow teacher that you are behind on marking, but you may not want to advertise that to your Head of Department. If you had a hectic weekend and didn't plan your Monday morning lessons properly, again, don't put your foot in it. As Heads of Department are not in your lesson all the time, they often make silent judgments based upon how you come across. Don't give them reasons to misjudge you. Aside from that, remember that a relaxed teacher is a good teacher so relax and be yourself.

Don't mistake familiarity for friendship

You may be on friendly terms with your Head of Department, but know that most Heads of Department will not allow this friendship to compromise your professionalism. Don't assume that your mate will let you off a book scrutiny or an observation, and don't take it personally if your mate is the one who (metaphorically speaking) has to put a knife in you if you screw up. They have a job to do, as do you. Don't lose sight of either.

Support them

If your Head of Department makes a request you can accommodate, then do so. If you see them clearly struggling with a task and you have the time and resources to be of assistance, then lend a hand, even if it's not within your remit. Remember that supportive behaviour breeds supportive behaviour, and your Head of Department is more likely to support you in future if they know that you are a team player. A good Head of Department will have your back. Give them reasons to have your back: support them.

With Senior Leaders

In most school set-ups, senior leaders are not involved in your daily lives. You may only see them in the odd departmental meeting, briefings, in the staffroom, just in passing, or of course if they are observing your lesson. Senior leaders form their judgements based upon the testimony of others (staff and pupils) as well as the vibes you give off. In addition to following much of the advice that relates to your Head of Department, take note of the small gems that follow:

Mind your language

Depending on your school, you may consider this obvious or ridiculous, but hear me out. Strictly speaking, swearing in the workplace is unprofessional. Most teachers and Heads of Department don't give a shit if you do, but senior leaders will most likely frown on it even though they probably won't comment on it. It's just safer to censor yourself around them.

Watch what you say

If you are under a lot of stress, you may end up unprofessionally venting your frustrations about pupil behaviour, for example. Be careful what you say in front of senior leaders. Your colleagues may lend you a supportive ear, but unprofessional behaviour is still unprofessional behaviour. Senior leaders may call you out on it if you're unlucky.

Don't stress

Try not to appear as if you are overly stressed or aren't coping well, even if you are going through a tough period. Smile and appear confident and in control wherever possible. Your body language should display that you enjoy your job and are an enthusiastic teacher. Don't talk about how your year 11 target grades are too high and there is no way they will be achieved. System bashing will score you no points. Have an aura of positivity.

Be yourself

You don't have to turn into a big bumbling ball of nerves, nor do you have to kiss ass just because you are talking to a senior leader. Relax, just modify your behaviour slightly if you need to.

With Support Staff

As a teacher you will most definitely rely on the help of support staff to get you through the working week. A strong relationship with them is therefore crucial if you are to reach your potential as a teacher. The good thing is that it actually doesn't take too much effort from your side to maintain a solid supportive relationship with support staff.

Always ask, never tell

The biggest complaint against teachers from support staff is that they are often told what to do as if they are to wait around at every teacher's beck and call. They complain about a hierarchy in which they are at the bottom. If you want support staff to do you those extra favours, or to save your life when it needs saving, then it is essential for you to treat them with respect: ditch the hierarchy. Speak to them as equals and remember that, just like you, they too are overworked, underpaid and have to prioritise. If you want to be higher on their priority list, always ask. Never tell.

Grovel

If you make a mistake that they end up taking the punishment for, then you had better grovel. An example may be that you sent 1500 booklets for photocopying, and you accidently gave the wrong ones, so they had to be done again. Or you may have requested and then later cancelled a complex science practical, which the technician spent a lot of time preparing in your room. In these and similar scenarios just own up and apologise. A peace offering of a tin of biscuits also wouldn't go amiss!

On the off chance that you do get a member of support staff who is regularly awkward or workshy, don't enter a confrontation. Just complain to their line manager. This aside, if you treat support staff as equals and don't mess them about too often, you will be higher on their priority list.

12.

Why It's All Worth It

Folks are usually about as happy as they make their minds up to be

- Abraham Lincoln

I came across the above quote when I was having what I think is referred to as an existential crisis during a very difficult NQT year. Cut to 11 years and four schools later, I genuinely believe this is right – a teacher's happiness is their decision. In this final chapter I aim to illustrate why I choose to be a happy teacher, and how you can too.

Teaching is fun

A few years ago, a colleague and I decided to go all out for the school charity and have a boxing match against each other. My colleague weighed 18 stone and I weighed 9 and a half stone. We both had boxing experience and it was the deliberate ridiculousness of the imbalance of our weight that incited us to do this, not only for the charity, but for the kids' entertainment also. I remember that we actually weren't allowed to call it a 'fight', however. We had to call it a 'charity boxing tournament'. The school was worried about being seen as promoting violence, typical eh? We spent weeks training together and choreographing this 'fight' that we were determined to make look real. I had to get used to taking some hard shots, although my colleague insisted he was just tapping me. The 'fight' day was amazing. The gym was full of pupils, we both had our own entry music and we had a sixth former acting as referee. Neither of us was willing to lose in front of the pupils, so we pre-planned a double knockout. The kids absolutely loved it! They were shaking hands with us afterwards and you could see that they had a deep sense of respect and admiration for us. I think that this is one of those moments I will absolutely never ever forget, and I doubt the kids will either. In fact, knowledge of the 'fight' actually followed me to the school I taught at after that!

It is rare, if not impossible, to have this kind of fun in other jobs. Teaching is fun. Embrace the fun! Banter with the kids, banter in the staffroom. You don't have to wait for novel events: your daily practice can be fun if you choose for it to be. See the humour in every situation and your stress will decrease, while your happiness will increase. See the humour even if it's difficult to do so. Just last week I was explaining a concept to my class and every time I shifted my position, the kids would laugh. They did not tell me what they were laughing at no matter how much I asked them, and the laughing eventually became disruptive so I had to reprimand them. Only then did they tell me that the reason they were engaging in this synchronised laughter, was because every time I moved in and out of the light, it would make my bald head look shiny then dull, shiny then dull, shiny then dull. I chose to find this funny and carry on with my lesson. Avoiding the light of course!

Teachers are thanked and appreciated

Teachers who report job dissatisfaction often cite the lack of praise or recognition from school leaders as a reason. The solution to this, I believe, is simple: don't rely on extrinsic factors for motivation. Your managers are your managers; they are not your pupils. Teaching is only a thankless profession if you are looking to the wrong sources for approval – not that you should beg for anyone's approval, but I'm sure you take the point.

I learnt pretty early on that the best source of job satisfaction is from the pupils you teach. Of course it is inevitable that some pupils will outright resent you, the school, and the education system in its entirety, but most won't. The ones that do thank you, however, are not always obvious with their thanks: they are not going to show up to your lesson with an apple and ask you what wonderful concepts you're going to teach them today. No. But they will thank you in subtle, and indeed not-so-subtle ways.

I can recall a time when as an NQT, I got observed by a Deputy Head with a very chatty, although not disrespectful, group. I struggled the whole year to get the class quiet and rarely managed to do so, so naturally I was shitting myself when I received the email to tell me about the observation. I recall planning, checking my plan, planning again, losing sleep, and expressing my concerns about behaviour to my mentor who would just tell me to relax and stop stressing. He always had faith in me. At the time I never understood why.

When the observation began, the Deputy Head arrived and I became visibly nervous. I remember a charismatic girl quietly saying 'Sir, your brow… are you ok?'

She was referring to the sweat on my forehead as I was handing out the mini whiteboards, which, to add insult to injury, I dropped while handing out and had to pick up in the middle of the observation. Another girl called me over and said 'Sir, is Mr Smith watching you?', to which I discreetly nodded. 'Oh ok, I'll be good then' she replied. I can recall the pupils being absolutely silent and holding on to my every word when I was explaining the structure of the atom, something I had never seen them do.

Now you may argue that it was the fear of the Deputy Head that impeded the pupils' chatter, however, I can assure you that this was not the case. Pupils at this particular school had no fear of authority whatsoever. They behaved out of respect for me alone. Either that, or they just felt sorry for me. Either way, it is moments like this that not only make me feel warm and fuzzy inside, but remind me that as a teacher, I matter: what I do is appreciated. Yes, this class was disruptive normally, but that was most probably because they were more interested in each other than they were in my science lessons (which were admittedly probably a bit crap at the time). When push came to shove, they appreciated me and did not embarrass me when they so easily could have. I mattered to them and this was their way of subtly showing their appreciation.

As a teacher, never lose sight of the fact that you are appreciated. As said previously, kids are not going to thank you on a regular basis, but if you look closely, the signs that they are thankful to you, without actually thanking you, are ever present.

When a kid says 'Hello' to you in the corridor or noses into your personal life, that's his way of thanking you. When a class complains that they've had a cover teacher for too long, that's their way of thanking you. I think the most paradoxical display of thanks I ever had was not too long ago when a very lazy trainee took over one of my classes.

One of the naughty boys in the class quietly said to me 'Sir, when can we have you back? She can't control us'. It was as if he subconsciously knew that he was naughty and that he needed a good teacher to manage his behaviour. It was his way of asking me to save him from himself.

Another time I bumped into a girl I taught when she was in year 10 and who had now begun university. Within 30 seconds of speaking to me, she told me that she still uses UV protection on her skin to avoid wrinkles, even if it's not a sunny day. Then I remembered that it was me that told her that the two main factors that cause wrinkles are smoking and sunlight. She quoted this back to me as if I just told her yesterday. This was her way of thanking me for positively impacting her life.

I recently went back to my old boxing gym and bumped into a pupil, now 18, who I taught when he was in year 7. I was then an NQT and ran a boxing club for pupils and he was one of them. So not only was I his first ever boxing coach, I was also his first ever science teacher. And guess what? Not only was he continuing the boxing, but he was also studying A-level sciences. He and his friend then told me I was a 'sick geeza'. I think this was their way of thanking me.

There are many more examples I could give, as well as many thank you cards, gifts and so on. A bunch of pupils once even nominated me for a teacher award. The rewards body sent me a card to congratulate me for being nominated, but two weeks later they sent me an email to tell me that I hadn't been successful in winning. Oh well.

Teachers matter. Everyone you know can tell you about the teachers they had at school, and they can attribute something of their character or thought processes to a teacher. You are part of the making of a person. What a brilliant and privileged position to be in! Your university friends may be earning more money than you, but their name will be forgotten as soon as a robot that can do their job is invented, if not before. Your pupils will remember you for a lifetime. Subtly and not so subtly, they do thank you. So what other thanks is needed than from those whose lives you are improving?

Camaraderie

Psychologists claim that turning one's attention away from the self and towards others has a positive impact on happiness. The person whose inner voice says 'What can I do for you?' rather than 'What can I get out of this?' will become the happier person. By helping young people for 55 hours a week, we are already in the first category and this does not even take into account camaraderie between staff.

There is not a single success I have had as a teacher for which I cannot attribute much of the credit to other colleagues. For example, every time I have been successful in job interviews, one of the reasons is because other teachers helped me plan the interview lesson. Teachers like to help – it may be because we love the sound of our own voice – but we still like to help and aiding others builds camaraderie, which is essential for one's happiness.

Any well-managed school will have staff who are supportive of each other, almost like troops on a

131

battlefield. Not the 'you scratch my back, I'll scratch yours' kind of support, but a genuine sense of concern for fellow colleagues. My theory is that because of all of the external pressures, teachers have developed a kind of siege mentality: it's us against them so we have to stick together. It is usually the case that the more difficult the school, for example inner city, low attainment, low Ofsted grading, the stronger the camaraderie. Staff at these schools have good humour and are sociable, supportive and friendly. I have known staff who have left difficult schools to teach at 'easier' schools (suburban, high attaining, although these are not necessarily easier) only to return to the more difficult school after just one term. Why? Because they found them boring! Staff only spoke to each other when necessary and there just wasn't a sense of togetherness. Teachers kept their heads down and did their own thing. The Christmas do would be dead, Friday football would only have about 6 teachers and there was very little socialising in or outside of work.

Camaraderie is among the most enjoyable aspects of teaching. I can recall a few years ago when my school got the dreaded Ofsted phone call, and a colleague literally ran up and down the corridor opening everybody's door telling them to check their email. The Head called a whole school meeting at the end of the day and gave us a motivational speech. This was a good Headteacher who really did have the ability to motivate us by giving us confidence rather than causing us stress. She said the school was going to be open late, then she got the Deputy and Assistant Heads to knock on all of our doors to ask us if we needed anything. Our Head of Department called a meeting for us and we were all keen to help each other. We were even ringing each other at 1am to swap resources. After this we felt like a force to be reckoned with and were almost looking forward to Ofsted's arrival.

When I left that school, the Headteacher gave me a personal leaving card. She was a Headteacher who knew exactly how to be fun, familiar, and still get the most out of her staff. I had formed a good relationship with her, and although she was sad to lose me, she still put in a good word for me at my new school. Another Headteacher once drove me all the way home in the snow because I was a broke-ass NQT without even a driving license, let alone a car.

In conclusion, make a decision to be a happy teacher. It can be a struggle at times when you are working through a bottomless pile of marking, deleting irrelevant emails, or defending yourself vehemently for something you forgot to do! You are only human, and it's a good thing you are, because you have the ability to compartmentalise. Compartmentalisation can be defined as the mind's ability to deal with conflicting internal standpoints. Compartmentalisation helps soldiers put aside traumatic events during times of war in order to maintain focus on the battlefield. Marking books is not as traumatic, but to be a happy teacher you must compartmentalise: you are there because you are appreciated, you have fun, and you enjoy the camaraderie. Focus on those three things. Be a happy teacher.

Notes

1. Mark Easton, 'Our children need time not stuff',
    BBC, September 13 2011,
    http://www.bbc.co.uk/news/uk-14899148

2. Jay Belsky 'Parent to child: I am NOT your friend
    (nor should I be)', *Psychology Today- Family
    Affair,* September 12 2008,
    https://www.psychologytoday.com/blog/family-
    affair/200809/parent-child-i-am-not-your-friend-
    nor-should-i-be

3. Sally Weale, 'Four in 10 new teachers quit within
    a year', *The Guardian,* March 31 2015,
    https://www.theguardian.com/education/2015/
    mar/31/four-in-10-new-teachers-quit-within-a-
    year

4. Hannah Richardson, 'More than 50% of teachers
    in England 'plan to quit in the next two years'',
    The Guardian, October 4 2015,
    http://www.bbc.co.uk/news/education-34426598

5. 'What hours do teachers really work?', *BBC,* April
    19 2014, http://www.bbc.co.uk/news/education-
    27087942

6. Christopher Bergland, Cortisol: "Why 'the stress hormone' is public enemy no. 1", *Psychology Today,* January 22 2013, https://www.psychologytoday.com/blog/the-athletes-way/201301/cortisol-why-the-stress-hormone-is-public-enemy-no-1#

7. Natasha Turner, '5 natural ways to increase your serotonin levels', *Chatelaine,* March 17 2017, http://www.chatelaine.com/health/wellness/natural-ways-to-increase-your-serotonin-levels/

8. Haroon Siddique, 'Britons missing an hour's sleep every night, says report', *The Guardian,* April 1 2016, https://www.theguardian.com/lifeandstyle/2016/apr/01/uk-hours-sleep-night-report-average-royal-society-for-public-health

9. Judy Willis, 'Teacher's guide to sleep – and why it matters', *The Guardian,* November 11 2014, https://www.theguardian.com/teacher-network/teacher-blog/2014/nov/11/good-night-teacher-guide-sleep

10. Ann Pietrangelo, 'The effects of sleep deprivation on the body', *Healthline,* August 19 2014, http://www.healthline.com/health/sleep-deprivation/effects-on-body

11. 'Study calls for smartphones to have 'bedtime mode'', *NHS Choices*, November 16 2015, http://www.nhs.uk/news/2015/11November/Pages/Study-calls-for-smartphones-and-tablets-to-have-bedtime-mode.aspx

12. Jacob Schor, 'Cherry juice supplies melatonin and improves sleep', *Natural Medicine Journal*, May 2012, http://www.naturalmedicinejournal.com/journal/2012-05/cherry-juice-supplies-melatonin-and-improves-sleep

13. Molly Webster, 'Can you catch up on lost sleep?', *Scientific American,* May 6 2008, https://www.scientificamerican.com/article/fact-or-fiction-can-you-catch-up-on-sleep/

14. Amy S. Wharton, 'The Psychology of Emotional Labour', *Annual Review of Sociology,* August 11 2009.
    http://www.annualreviews.org/doi/abs/10.1146/annurev-soc-070308-115944

15. Manshi Kohli, 'How exercise boosts confidence', *India Times,* November 20 2011,
    http://www.indiatimes.com/health/tips-tricks/how-exercise-boosts-confidence-238523.html

16. Jennifer Warner, 'Exercise fights fatigue, boosts energy', *Webmd,* November 3 2006,
    http://www.webmd.com/diet/news/20061103/exercise-fights-fatigue-boosts-energy

17. 'Physical activity guidelines for adults', *NHS Choices,* July 11 2015,
    http://www.nhs.uk/Livewell/fitness/Pages/physical-activity-guidelines-for-adults.aspx

18. 'Leafy green vegetables', *The Science of Eating,*
    http://thescienceofeating.com/vegetables/best-leafy-green-vegetables/

19. Martha Purdue, 'If coffee is a stimulant, why does it make me sleepy?', *Drinkal,* December 16 2016, https://www.drinkal.com/why-does-coffee-make-me-sleepy/#The_Sugar_Rush_Effect

20. Dr. Carl J. Brandt (Based on text by Brandt; reviewed by Jeni Worden), 'Vitamins and minerals – what do they do?', *Netdoctor,* September 26 2016, http://www.netdoctor.co.uk/healthy-eating/a10801/vitamins-and-minerals-what-do-they-do/

21. Sarah Boseley, 'Working long hours increases stroke risk, major study finds', *The Guardian,* August 20 2016, https://www.theguardian.com/lifeandstyle/2015/aug/20/working-longer-hours-increases-stroke-risk

22. Lawrence Robinson, Melinda Smith, & Jeanne Segal, 'Laughter is the best medicine', *Helpguide,* April 2017, https://www.helpguide.org/articles/emotional-health/laughter-is-the-best-medicine.htm

23. Sarah Marsh, 'It's official, teachers must relax over Christmas to avoid burnout', *The Guardian,* December 17 2015, https://www.theguardian.com/teacher-network/2015/dec/17/teachers-relax-christmas-avoid-burnout

24. 'Bullying and harassment, advice for individuals', *Health and Safety Executive,* http://www.hse.gov.uk/stress/furtheradvice/bullyingindividuals.htm

25. 'Secret teacher: bullies lurk in the staffroom too', *The Guardian,* November 16 2013, https://www.theguardian.com/teacher-network/teacher-blog/2013/nov/16/secret-teacher-bullies-staffroom

Printed in Poland
by Amazon Fulfillment
Poland Sp. z o.o., Wrocław